WEALTH
UNBROKEN

GROWING WEALTH UNINTERRUPTED BY MARKET CRASHES, TAXES, AND EVEN DEATH

REBECCA WALSER
JD, LLM, CFP®

Wealth Unbroken: Growing Wealth Uninterrupted By Market Crashes, Taxes And Even Death

Copyright © 2018 Rebecca Walser

Published by Atlantic Publishing Group, Inc.
1405 SW 6th Avenue • Ocala, Florida 34471 • Phone 352-622-1825 • Fax 352-622-1875
Website: www.atlantic-pub.com • Email: sales@atlantic-pub.com
SAN Number: 268-1250

Library of Congress Cataloging-in-Publication Data

Names: Walser, Rebecca, 1974- author.
Title: Wealth unbroken : growing wealth uninterrupted by market crashes, taxes and even death / Rebecca Walser, JD,
   LLM, CFP.
Description: Ocala, Florida : Atlantic Publishing, Inc, [2017] | Includes
   bibliographical references and index.
Identifiers: LCCN 2017047796| ISBN 9781620235164 (alk. paper) | ISBN
   1620235161 (alk. paper)
Subjects: LCSH: Finance, Personal--United States. | Retirement income--United
   States--Planning. | Wealth--United States.
Classification: LCC HG179 .W37 2017 | DDC 332.024/010973--dc23
LC record available at https://lccn.loc.gov/2017047796

Printed in the United States
Year of First Printing: 2018

PROJECT MANAGER: Danielle Lieneman • dlieneman@atlantic-pub.com
COVER, JACKET DESIGN & INTERIOR LAYOUT: Antoinette D'Amore • addesign@videotron.ca

DISCLAIMER

While great efforts have been taken to provide accurate and current information regarding the covered material, neither Walser Wealth, Walser Capital Group, nor Rebecca Walser is responsible for any errors or omissions, or for the results obtained from the use of this information.

The name *'Wealth Unbroken, Growing Wealth Uninterrupted By Market Crashes, Taxes, And Even Death'* is a marketing concept and does not guarantee or imply that changes will be made to your wealth. The act of purchasing any book, course, or financial product holds no such guarantees.

The ideas, suggestions, general principles and conclusions presented here are subject to local, state and federal laws and regulations and revisions of same, and are intended for informational purposes only. All information in this report is provided "as is," with no guarantee of completeness, accuracy, or timeliness regarding the results obtained from the use of this information. And without warranty of any kind, express or implied, including, but not limited to warranties of performance, merchantability, and fitness for a particular purpose. Your use of this information is at your own risk.

You assume full responsibility and risk of loss resulting from the use of this information. Rebecca Walser, Walser Wealth, and Walser Capital Group will not be liable for any direct, special, indirect, incidental, consequential, or punitive damages or any other damages whatsoever, whether in an action based upon a statute, contract, tort (including, but not limited to negligence), or otherwise, relating to the use of this information.

In no event will Rebecca Walser, Walser Wealth, Walser Capital Group, or their related companies, partnerships, or corporations, or the partners, agents, or employ-

Table of Contents

CHAPTER 2:
Why You Love the Law
(Even If You Don't Know It Yet)

CHAPTER 3:
The Infection of Elitism

CHAPTER 4:
America's Money

PART 2:
Why We Aren't
Where We Should Be

CHAPTER 5:
The Way America Retires Now

CHAPTER 8:
Fundamental Flaw #3 –
Debt & Interest, Retirement & Savings Gap **129**

CHAPTER 11:
Building Your Legacy.. **183**

Foreword

This book holds within it the answers many Americans have about their futures.

Wealth Unbroken means that you can grow your wealth continuously, uninterrupted by market crashes, taxes, or even death. By precisely following the blueprint laid out in this book, you can put yourself in a position most Americans will never achieve…true financial independence.

I was so impressed with the depth of the content of this book that even I learned a few new things… and I've been in the finance industry for over 15 years.

Take the time to read the book, take control of your wealth, and most importantly act on it. You'll be glad you did.

Brett Kitchen

Dedication

For my sail,
for taking me
to heights
yet unknown...

WHERE WE ARE NOW AND WHY WE ARE HERE

CHAPTER

1

My Humble Beginnings

100 Men

In 2000, the Office of Research, Evaluation, and Statistics – a division of the Social Security Administration - compiled a study and found that for every 100 people in the workforce, the following average outcomes would exist at age 65:

- Approximately 16 out of 100 would not live to reach age 65.
- 66 of those who reach age 65 will have incomes at or below $20,000 annually, which will force them to become dependent upon their children, the government, or charity, or it will require them to continue working in some capacity beyond age 65.
- 14 of those who reach age 65 will have incomes in excess of $30,000 annually, giving them the ability to be financially independent but without a substantial quality of life.

- Four of those who reach age 65 will have an income in excess of $50,000 annually, making them financially independent with a substantial quality of life.

Can you imagine? America, one of the richest countries on the face of the Earth over the entire course of history, and only four out of 100 people will actually achieve financial success in retirement. Granted this study is dated at the turn of the millennium, but the results are no less shocking.

Out of 100 people, where do you see yourself? Which category does your life or will your life fall into? Where do you want it to fit if you have not yet reached age 65?

I know my answer, and I know my clients' answers.

I am writing this book because of the results from studies like this one. America has been building wealth inadequately for a while now, but especially over the last 40+ years.

You have bought this book because you want to be among the four out of 100 that actually make it, that actually do it right, that know that there just must be a better way.

Because you are right – there is.

This book will show you why 96 out of 100 Americans will fail.

There will be naysayers, doubters, and pessimists all around you. They will attack from all sides and try to tear down what you know within yourself to be true.

But, you see, they are a part of the majority, the 96 out of 100 that are doing it wrong.

If what you discover and believe to be factual turns out to be true, it means that they are a part of the 96 that will fail… and they will be unwilling to accept that. So, they will try to disprove and negate what you know to be true already.

If they were doing it right, if America was doing it right, then the numbers would be reversed and 96, the majority, would be successful; only a tiny fraction of people would be failing.

But the whole of America is in fact failing and getting it wrong. For those of you who have eyes to see and ears to hear, this book is written for you.

Flipping the Switch

It all began when I was very, very young. One of my earliest childhood memories is about money.

I walked into the bathroom and flipped on the light switch.

Nothing happened.

Huh? I thought...

What's wrong with the light? Why won't it come on?

So, I switched it off and then back on.

Off. On. Off. On.

Nothing.

I found my Mom and told her the light was broken. My parents looked at each other, sat me down, and gave me my first lesson about money.

The lesson really was quite simple. "There are things in life called bills and it takes money to pay those bills. If you don't have enough money, you cannot pay all of your bills. And if you do not pay your bills, the lights won't come on."

My parents hadn't done anything wrong. They just didn't have the money.

I remember the power being cut several times throughout my childhood. My family's struggles with money gave me my appreciation of finance. At an early age, I became passionate about (and a little obsessed with) finances. I wanted to learn everything there was to know about finance — how to save money, grow it, and manage it.

My humble beginnings made me into the person I am today. From the moment I flipped that light switch, I have spent my entire life focused on finance, economics, wealth, taxes on wealth, and building financial legacies. That bathroom light did not turn on... but my passion for everything financial did.

What Does It Mean to Build a Financial Legacy?

What does it really mean to build a financial legacy? In what I call the *New Normal* of today's economy, what does it mean to truly prepare to leave your family — and those whose lives you've touched — better off financially?

I'm not talking about retirement. That's important too, but what does it mean to truly leave your loved ones better off financially because you were a part of their lives?

I am Rebecca Walser, a wealth strategist and tax attorney. I'm in love with America's freedoms. It is my passion — my mission — to convey to as many as possible the importance of taking control of your financial future.

You see, when it comes to wealth creation, management, and building financial legacies, most of America is doing it wrong; most of America is using retirement tools that are just NOT right for today's economic environment.

I am so very enthusiastic about getting it right. I am obsessed with helping people avoid the wealth management and retirement traps that our financial industry is riddled with.

Working with all sorts of people — people of family and generational wealth, entrepreneurs and business owners, and those who are just starting out — has been a true blessing for me because I have seen how the system works from all angles and perspectives. I know what works and what doesn't, and I want to make sure you are making the best decisions for the lifestyle you want and for the legacy you want to leave behind. I want to make a personal impact on your financial well-being.

The Wrong Path

When it comes to wealth management and building financial legacies, most of America is headed down the wrong path.

Why? America is at the dawn of a new era — a *'New Normal'* — if you will.

No longer are stable financial markets the norm.

No longer is it solely true that the way America goes, so goes the world.

No longer is your career path predictable.

No longer is working for the same company for the whole of your career (and having a guaranteed pension for the rest of your life) to be expected.

And in this new world of technological innovation, no longer are the careers of today just for the heavily debt-laden, college-educated.

The global impact of the *New Normal* is already here.

Financially speaking, most of us have utilized retirement vehicles that just don't work anymore. Sure, they serve the institutions and advisors who are recommending them, but when it comes to actually supporting you in retirement, more often than not, they will fall far short. They were designed using old market models of stable, sustained growth and have not caught up with new market patterns of extreme high highs followed by severe low lows.

We are also, of course, up against a ticking tax time bomb. Our debt is at an all-time, almost unfathomable high. That, in addition to our nation's largest generation all retiring at the same time, places us in the worst fiscal position of our nation's history. Given all that, do you really think taxes will actually *decrease* in the future? Since 1935, financial institutions, traditions and history, and even plain old circumstance and the occasional "accident" have defined the way America creates wealth. Most Americas have been convinced to invest in ways that do not serve their best interests. If you pay attention, you can see the warning signs and make valuable, lasting changes to your financial future.

If you pay attention, you can take control.

What Are You Leaving Behind?

It's never too late to build your financial legacy. No matter what stage of life you're in, there is going to be *something* in this book for you.

If you're young and just beginning to build your wealth, this book will show you the impact of getting started early and the difference 10 years of investment time can make.

For everyone who's already fallen into the traditional retirement traps, this book will show you a way out and how to make the changes you need to get more out of your retirement.

And for everyone in their golden years, whether you want to simply maintain your lifestyle in retirement or create a financial legacy for your family, this book will help you too.

I am reminded of a recent client who was legacy-minded, had $4 million in liquid capital, and nine grandchildren of varying ages one to 13.

He wanted to use the annual gift tax exclusion of $14,000 per year, per person to gift to each of his grandchildren for the next 10 years. At $126,000 a year (nine grandchildren, remember), the total needed for the gifting strategy was $1.26 million.

Now, what if I told you that through specialized planning, we are able to turn that $1.26 million fund into $45 million?

Sound amazing?

It is.

But it's only possible if you utilize the right tools.

We leveraged his wealth and planned the legacy he wanted, and this family will never be the same. Our country was designed so Americans can prosper. Armed with the right knowledge, anything is possible!

As an experienced wealth strategist and tax attorney, I am passionate about helping you prosper. I am passionate about helping you build your financial legacy.

So, what are you going to leave behind?

My Ticket Out

Because of my modest background, at an early age I learned the value of money and the importance of wealth accumulation.

I wanted to take control of my financial future, and in order to do that, I learned to rely on my brain. My ticket was an education.

I was the lucky though. Not because school came easy to me or I was one of those super geniuses that never studied and still got straight A's.

I did well because I worked hard. Those straight A's took a lot of work. I was lucky because I genuinely loved both math and economics. These topics were (and still are) super exciting to study, learn, and understand.

So many people do not understand anyone that naturally loves math, economics, or finance, but it really is very simple.

You see, math isn't fallible; it has no gray area, unlike the law, which often has to be interpreted by a court. Math is pure. It is binary. It is either black or white, on or off. It never lies or misleads.

The best example of what I mean actually comes from the movie *Titanic*.

After the boat strikes the iceberg and people are running around going crazy, you see the engineer, Thomas Andrews, calmly walking to retrieve the boat's blueprints and then walking into the captain's quarters. He ignores the passenger who proudly states that the boat cannot sink and methodically rolls the blueprints out onto the table.

> **Thomas Andrews:** *She can stay afloat with the first four compartments breached but not five. Not five. She goes down by the head, the water will spill over the bulkheads, from one to the next, back and back there's no stopping it.*
> **Capt. Smith:** *The pumps, we open the doors.*
> **Thomas Andrews:** *The pumps buy you time! But minutes only. From this moment there's no matter what to do. Titanic will founder.*
> **Bruce Ismay:** *But this ship can't sink.*
> **Thomas Andrews:** *She's made of iron sir! I assure you she can! And she will. It is a mathematical certainty.*[1]

That my friends, that certainty, that pureness of exactness, is why math is such a beautiful thing. Math is one of the few things in life you can count on.

Leveraging the power of math and economics combined produces the field of finance, the industry where I have chosen to dedicate my life.

This passion led me to graduate summa cum laude with my Bachelor's in Business Finance. The last semester of my senior year, I was fortunate enough to begin my first real job working for PricewaterhouseCoopers (PwC), a renowned international professional services firm.

Before I knew it, I was promoted and worked for a boss based in London. Consequently, the job required a lot of international travel (which seemed extremely glamorous to a 22-year-old). It made me feel like I had arrived, like I had really made it... I was loving every minute of it.

Scariest Moment of My Life

As fun and exciting as international travel was, I would be lying if I told you that it didn't get old. The experience I gained was invaluable — I don't want to minimize that — but after years and years of traveling, I was getting tired. I was getting burnt out.

And then I boarded a night flight from Orlando to London, never expecting to have the scariest moment of my life.

I was in business class of a 747, located in the upstairs nose, joined by only one other passenger who had been asleep since takeoff. I was very restless that flight and couldn't fall asleep. About three hours in the air, I started to hear a buzzing noise.

If you have ever had a terrifying event in your life, you will recognize that the first stage of something intense is denial.

When I first heard that buzzing sound, I convinced myself that there was nothing wrong. I went with that for a while until the buzzing became so loud that I had no choice but to deal with it. Almost in slow motion (as I remember it now), I was reaching forward to press the call button for the flight attendant when the loudest noise I'd ever heard boomed through the air...

"POP!"

And the plane was on fire two rows in front of me! I could not believe what was happening — it was all so surreal.

Then it hit me: I was three hours into an eight-hour flight... over the Atlantic Ocean!

The feeling of sheer and utter helplessness in that moment was unlike anything I had ever experienced in my life. I was totally and completely powerless, and all I could do was pray.

As I saw my life flashing before me, I thought to myself, "What am I doing? How did I get here? This job isn't worth it. I have too much life still to live."

Just as I started lamenting a life cut short, nine flight attendants were in the nose of the plane with fire extinguishers, hosing down every inch from all directions.

Just as quickly as it started, it was over; the fire was out.

As crazy as the fire itself was, what happened next remains just as vivid in my memory. One flight attendant had climbed on top of a seat to attack the flames from above. She climbed down from the top of the seat and, like the proper British woman she was, she straightened her scarf, pulled down her blouse, and re-tucked it into her skirt. She walked toward me cool, calm, and collected, as if she were walking on the stage of the Miss Universe pageant instead of away from an electric fire. She leaned over, wrapped her arm around my shoulders and said, "How about some wine?"

"Umm, yes please," I replied in a numb, shocked muffle.

Everything went back to normal... but the experience really shook me. I started thinking about my life and all the travel and knew it was time for a change. It was time to reconnect with American business.

That is the beauty of life, especially of life in America. Things change when *you* decide they will. How you will change those things always comes later, *but it is the choice to make a change that really means something, that really sets the change in motion.* These pivotal life moments happen when you realize that your entire life will forever change based on your decision in that moment. Those life-altering moments are the ones that count.

I went on to have more corporate experiences in finance and even met my husband along the way at the global networking division of IBM, which was acquired by AT&T.

I gained invaluable experience in real estate finance, and together, my husband and I were fortunate to be doing well enough that he left his corporate job and started his own business.

After a few years, his business had taken off, and I found myself dealing with a lot of lawyers for his company, whether for business contracts, employment contracts, trademark litigation and on and on. This opened an opportunity for me to marry my love of finance to the law, to go to law school and become an attorney.

To me it sounded like heaven. As you know I *love* math but I discovered that I also truly love the law. And if you believe as I believe — that what you become in life is truly up to you, that your destiny is yours to fulfill or not fulfill — then by the end of this book, I believe you will love the law too!

I was so fortunate to attend the University of Florida for my law degree, graduating with honors. I went even further and earned an advanced law degree in Taxation from New York University.

Those times were definitely a challenge and a major sacrifice for my young family, but perseverance is really what true champions are made of. Things that are worth achieving in life are often the very hardest things to achieve.

Too often it is just the sheer will and strength to persevere that most people are lacking. It holds them back from becoming all they want to become, all that they could become. I hope my journey will inspire my own children to always pursue their ultimate purpose in life — whatever that may be.

Fast Forward to Practicing Law

After graduating in New York, I returned to central Florida and worked at a boutique law firm practicing estate planning and tax law with private clients of substantial wealth.

And it was common for our clients to bring their financial advisors with them whenever they would come to our offices to meet with us regarding tax strategy and estate planning.

As a lawyer, my clients and their financial advisors were unaware of my background and years of financial experience.

The Boardroom

One day, I was visiting a client in their boardroom when I had an epiphany.

I was sitting on one side of the conference table with the client at the head of his table and his advisor on the other side. Listening to his financial advisor giving my client bad advice made my ears burn. I personally considered his advice awful, and I wanted, desperately, to save my client from it.

But neither my client nor his advisor were aware of my financial background, which made it so much worse. Here I was, qualified to help this man, and I was the only one in that room who knew it.

In that moment, I knew right then and there, that solely practicing law wasn't going to fulfill my destiny. I couldn't practice tax law in a silo. I needed to have my own practice where I could holistically practice both the tax side of law and the financial side of wealth building.

I wanted to work with financial tools designed to maximize wealth within the unique context of long-term legal tax minimization. I wanted to build *true generational wealth* in the most tax-advantaged ways possible.

So, I did what every entrepreneur has done before me. I built up the courage to eventually quit my steady job with the firm and took the leap of faith to go it alone. I was going out on my own to use my financial and legal skills to help people build real, lasting, generational wealth.

Don't let me sugar coat it. Accumulating wealth is not easy, especially in places where it doesn't yet exist.

But, working with all kinds of people at all different wealth levels, I can say with absolute certainty and confidence, that wealth is so much harder to build when you utilize the *wrong vehicles* in which to accumulate it; when you use the wrong design to start with.

Unfortunately, most of America is doing just that. They are simply doing what has been done for the last 40 years — what convention tells us is normal. Most Americans simply are not taking control.

These conventional methods could be financially dangerous because a perfect storm is brewing. Deciding to take control now could mean the difference between a successful financial future or one of failure, of being one of the four instead of one of the 96.

With my unique background and roots in both finance and the law, I see clearly now. By reading this book, my hope is that you will as well.

Why You Love the Law
(Even If You Don't Know It Yet)

M&Ms, Economics, and the Law

My first day of real property law cemented the importance of the law in my mind forever. My professor held up a clear bag filled with 75 colored chocolate M&M candies and said that each of the 100 students in my class wanted one candy, but that the candies could not be sub-divided. Life is not fair and all things are not equal, she explained.

She then continued, "How do we solve this problem?"

One student yelled out, "I'll buy mine," another said "I'll work for one," and on and on.

She responded by asking, "Well, first, what is the problem we have?"

She said "There's not enough, and you all proposed monetary solutions to solve this problem: 'I'll buy one,' 'I'll work for mine.' What we have is the basic economic problem of scarcity. In a world of finite, limited resources and unlimited needs and wants, the dilemma of how to distribute those limited resources is solved through the basic economic principles of supply and demand."

But then she pivoted, "but this class isn't *Economics 101*. It's *Real Property Law*, so *why* are we talking economics?"

She continued, "Economics is nothing without law. In fact, the law is what makes economics possible. What good would it do you to buy an M&M if no one in this room respected the fact that it was yours and yours alone?"

When everyone owns everything or no one owns anything, there is no such thing as supply and demand, so the law is at the core, the very foundation, in fact, of what makes economics a reality and makes the equilibrium between supply and demand possible."

Property rights provided through the law — specifically, the right to actually own something to the exclusion of all others, which is respected by all others — is what makes the economic equilibrium resolving all scarcity problems viable."

I knew that I loved finance and economics, but now it was clear how the law was such an integral part of making those disciplines a reality.

Our right to our own property is protected under our Constitution, and no one, including the government, can take that property from you without justifiable cause and recompense. You can buy something, have it titled in your name, and have exclusive rights to it.

The government might be able to tax you, but the law says that your property is exclusively yours. We take it for granted, but our American right to own property is simply not the same anywhere else in the world.

One of my favorite clients is from Croatia. She immigrated to the U.S. and married a business owner here. Given my past working internationally, I find her background and experience fascinating, and we often have stimulating conversations.

Thinking back, there is one conversation in particular that really struck a chord with me. We were discussing American entrepreneurship and I remember her saying, "Americans think this is the way it is everywhere but it's not like this over in Eastern Europe. It's just not."

I didn't really understand what she meant, so I asked her to explain.

"Over there, people just accept whichever station they were born into. If you were born poor, you will be poor for the rest of your life. Period. There is no '*American*' mentality that you can just get up and get out of your circumstances.

"In America, people are born into a society that knows that you can become whatever you want. As long as you are willing to work hard and keep at it, you have the ability to completely change your circumstances. Here, you can create something for yourself. Where I come from and around the world, it just isn't like that."

I wrinkled my nose and scrunched my face in thought. She was right. American history is wrought with rags-to-riches stories. Because of our Constitution, Americans have the ability to change their station in life simply because they decide to and because they have the perseverance, drive, and skills to.

But most of us take that for granted. We take for granted that we have a government that was established at its very foundation to protect the liberties and freedoms of its people, including the freedom to become whatever they want to be.

As corny as it sounds, it's true. No other country in the world has a government specifically designed around protecting the rights of its' people and their pursuit of happiness. That makes America exceptional.

I was speaking with a colleague of mine once, also a business owner, and he was more or less complaining about how intrusive the government had become with regulation and administrative expenses, and so on.

I stopped for a minute and shared my M&M story with him, explaining to him how I loved the law.

He responded by saying, "Rebecca, no business owner that I have ever talked with has had that perspective. They always see the law and regulation as a barrier to business, but you have just made me realize that our law is the reason I can have a business to start with — that's really amazing!"

I agree with his sentiments. When you realize the very American life we enjoy is because of America's exceptional, unique form of government, you can appreciate it in a brand new light. Doesn't it also make you want to be ever vigilant to protect our freedoms from any government regime that could become unduly restrictive, erecting barriers and burdens that creep from common sense protections to intrusions into our free society over time? These are the very reasons we revolted against our motherland, England, to start with!

The law is getting more and more restrictive each and every day. But without law, Americans, and the economy we love, simply aren't protected.

Really, it is commonplace now that many feel our nation has become an "administrative state" and rightfully so. But we should not be intimidated by this.

No, just the opposite.

Because of the unique structure of our Constitution and the almost paranoid protections our founding fathers created as they were leaving the restrictions of a repressive government, we have the ability to challenge our current status quo. We have the freedom to build wealth our own way.

I am passionate about that freedom. Being a lawyer, I cherish the exceptionalism of our American system of government, how special it is and how important it is to keep our liberties protected. Law school solidified my love for liberty and the law. I trust that you, too, see how you love the law because your right to create the life you desire and your ability to accumulate wealth are built upon it.

Mud Hut to Utilities Empire

I was recently honored to participate and speak at the Global Entrepreneurship Initiative at the United Nations. Of course, I was quite nervous and I did what every speaker does before any big event: I prepared by researching, and writing and rewriting my speech. I was scheduled to speak about what it means to be an entrepreneur and the impact that has had on my life.

Before it was my turn, the keynote speaker, Jeff Hoffman, the founder of Priceline.com, gave an incredible speech about the power of entrepreneurship that he had personally witnessed while traveling the world on behalf of President Obama's National Advisory Council on Innovation and Entrepreneurship.[2]

Hoffman shared that the president understood the positive economic effects of entrepreneurship, especially in third world countries, and how it pulls people out of poverty faster than anything else.

He then retold one of his experiences about how one day he received a letter from a man in Senegal, West Africa who had an idea and the journey this man took to make his idea a reality. This man had discovered a problem common to many Africans across the continent and its various countries.

But his circumstances were extremely limited, as he lived in a mud hut with no electricity. He walked to and from the fields for work every day, and if he wanted to use the internet, he would have to walk to the one place in town where he could get a connection.

But, even with all of this and despite his circumstances, he was dedicated to his entrepreneurial idea. He found a way: he took online classes from Stanford University through Coursera.com, studied TED talks, and created a business plan using slideshare.net, all to promote his brilliant idea of creating a utilities credit trading company where credits could transfer between companies and countries.

It wasn't long before seven African countries implemented his plan. Jeff then recounted flying out to meet this now multi-million dollar entrepreneurial businessman and how surreal it was to watch this man ride up in a luxury car entourage, through the very village in which he wrote his business plan. Until his idea took off, he had lived in a mud hut with no electricity, had worked in the fields, and had no formal education. But he had a dream and the will to pursue it in spite of his circumstances.

Now that's the power of entrepreneurship!

My Turn at the Mic

I was riveted by Hoffman's key note address, but the time had come for me to deliver my speech. I had been asked to write about what it means to be an entrepreneur. Naturally, I started with the term's definition.

But I *struggled* with this seemingly straightforward introduction. There was simply no definition that really captured the true essence of entrepreneurship.

Finally, I came across Austrian economist Joseph Schumpeter. He described capitalism as "the perennial gall of creative destruction," which is a free market's ceaseless movement towards more productivity, better products and services, more efficient work methods, and higher standards of living.[3]

That was it! Entrepreneurship was the gall of someone believing that they could create a better product or service and believing it so much that they are willing to risk their time, their money, their blood, sweat, and tears to make it happen.

Like Steve Jobs shaking up the computing world and building a better Walkman with the iPod; like Jeff Bezos saying that there is a better way to shop than physically going to a store or going to each individual store's website to buy a lot of different things, so he created Amazon; like Elon Musk believing that electricity is not just for golf carts, and on and on. That is entrepreneurship: the creative, destructive gall to do it better.

That is what it means to be an entrepreneur! You have the gall to believe there is a better way, you have the nerve to think that you are the one that can do it better, and you have the gumption to go out and try to make it happen!

Many may fail in the process, but they attempt, in every way possible, to make positive change happen. Entrepreneurs take control.

And those positive changes ripple through society. Entrepreneurs create jobs twice as quickly as established companies, driving economic growth.[4]

In developing countries, results like those are invaluable. Entrepreneurship elevates the quality of life for everyone involved, both domestically and abroad.

I believe that every human being is born with an innate desire to achieve success — whatever that might mean to them — and to make something of themselves. For the most part, "American Exceptionalism" has nothing to do with our people but has *everything* to do with the entrepreneurial support found within the U.S. Constitution. Our country's foundation was established to protect entrepreneurs and the "American Dream."

The founding fathers were entrepreneurs themselves. At a the time when the world was dominated by British Imperialism, our founding fathers dared to say, "Let's do something different. Let's do something *better.*"[5]

And it paid off. Their desire to build something new, something better, inspired the drafting of the Declaration of Independence and the

U.S. Constitution. The foundation they established paved the way for successful American entrepreneurship.

Challenging the Wisdom of Convention

Perhaps you are wondering why we are discussing the law and how America is unique in the world in a book about wealth creation. Well, that answer is easy: you should know that you have been born into great opportunity in this country, opportunity that is there for those who choose to take it. You may not feel that way given your own personal circumstances. Perhaps you do not have the financial means you want or don't have the support and encouragement to pursue a dream. But remember that simply by where you are in the world, you ARE empowered to take control of your own life, your own destiny, and that is something that billions of people do not have. America is set apart in that way, and it is something that I never want to forget or take for granted. And remember: if a man living in a mud hut without electricity or an education can do it in Africa, then why not you? I love the quote, "If it is to be, then it is up to me." Your destiny is yours to make.

I have been truly blessed. Not only am I passionate about my profession, but I get to work with so many different types of people. Through my work, I have been exposed to many unique perspectives and lifestyles.

Knowing how the law works, especially as to how it pertains to taxes, has allowed me to try and make a positive impact on the financial well-being of all Americans by writing this book. It allows me to help my clients take control of their wealth.

"Challenging The Wisdom Of Convention" is the byline of my practice's mission statement. Most Americans are building wealth the wrong way out of habit and out of convention. Through this book, I encourage you to challenge those old, outdated conventions and choose, instead, to build your wealth strategically.

Building intergenerational wealth for you and your family is possible, and if you didn't believe that to be true, then you wouldn't be spending your time reading my book. How you leverage the unique and empowering laws of this country to build your financial legacy remains to be seen. It's all up to you.

The Infection of Elitism

Security at the Oscars

Every year, around the beginning of spring, Hollywood's elite gather to celebrate the Academy Awards.

The event attracts film professionals from around the globe and, as it's typically attended by film and television's biggest stars, the event gets a lot of public attention, too.

Precise measures are taken to protect these entertainment behemoths. The event is held at the Dolby Theater, formerly known as the Kodak Theatre, right in the middle of Hollywood.

Traffic is stopped. Only vehicles with parking passes are allowed within a mile of the shopping complex hosting the theater.

When the guests arrive, they are greeted with the protection of roughly 500 police officers. But before they can reach the exclusive red carpet, they have to pass through a three-tiered security system.[6] We're talking about perimeters within perimeters within perimeters.

Or you could say, borders within borders within borders.

The Rationalization of Scarcity

Economics is the rationalization and balancing of scarcity. We will always have scarcity. We will always have finite money and finite resources and an unlimited demand for each.

Hollywood elites, too, are finite. There are only so many of them. Therefore, they are an excellent example of the economic principle of scarcity. The city of Los Angeles allocates extra resources for the elites' protection during awards shows. Taxpayers in Los Angeles pay to keep the Hollywood elites safe. They pay for borders.

I'm a lawyer. When it comes to approaching arguments, I take a disinterested, logical approach. I have been trained to examine problems from all sides. I know how to approach arguments from multiple angles.

For me, borders are logical, not political. They make sense. Because economics creates borders around finite resources that our Constitution was written to protect, economics is a blind equalizer.

Borders are necessary. While it may be a nice ideal, we simply cannot all share everything. There just simply isn't enough to go around.

America is a perfect example of that. We are the greatest nation on earth, but if we want to stay that way, if we want to protect everything that makes our nation unique and unrivaled, we *need* borders. Our resources, both physical and financial, are finite.

Economics protects those resources and law protects economics. It all works hand in hand.

Many Hollywood elite seem quick to shout for "open borders" but are they willing to play along? Are they too, willing to knock down their walls and their barriers? Are they willing to live alongside the common man? Is it logical to listen to the person speaking on the virtues of open borders from a guarded estate?

Tucker Carlson and the Feminist

Not everyone can have everything... and not everyone can be supported. It's just not possible.

For a stark example, take the transgender and feminist movements as a metaphor for scarcity and economics.

Sometime last year, I was watching an episode of the Tucker Carlson show. He was interviewing a feminist group leader when they began to discuss the transgender movement.

She stated that, as a feminist, she didn't know how to respond to it. She didn't know how to be an ally.

She then explained that women had to work hard to earn the right to vote. They had to work hard (and are still working hard) to earn equal representation and equal pay in the workplace. And based on their difficult efforts over many, many years, they had won many battles and had achieved numerous government grants and special programs for women that equate to millions and millions of dollars — all designed to help make up for the inequalities women have experienced for decades.

This feminist made the point that in the transgender community, from her perspective as a feminist fighting for women's rights, a man identifying as a woman trivialized all of their progress in the feminist movement. If a transgender person can be entitled to the status of a female simply because that is the gender that they believe they are, then what does it mean to be a woman? And what does it mean to be a feminist?

This is how this guest on Tucker Carlson explained the disconnect between her lifelong cause and the transgender movement.

How Can You Really Support Both?

Because I am a lawyer, I was trained to approach arguments objectively.

Without identifying with either side, I can see the inherent conflict in supporting both feminism and transgenderism.

Feminists believe there is no such thing as a "female brain." That women can do anything a man can do.

But transgender activists believe that people should assume the gender they identify with, even if it's different from the biology they were born with.

I'm not saying one group has a stronger argument than the other, I'm simply saying that philosophically, these ideals cannot exist simultaneously.

And so, how could both be supported at the same time?

The point I'm trying to make is that we can try to treat everyone equally, we can *really* try, but making everything perfectly equal and fair is simply not possible.

It just is not.

Protect What Makes Our Country Great

One elitist idea — in which everyone is accommodated, appeased, and treated specially — does not work. It is a simple matter of economics.

Economics is blind, making it as close to objective and fair as possible. It is also balanced out by the law. And because resources are finite, because money is finite, distributing those resources evenly would have catastrophic economic effects.

In the previous chapter, we talked about the foundation of the United States and its unique Constitution — the best on earth. We talked about entrepreneurship, economics, and the law. We talked about how our government and our laws are particularly geared toward protecting capitalism, entrepreneurs, and promoting entrepreneurship.

But even America, as prosperous and advantageous as it is, has limited resources.

If it came down to it, do you think we could accommodate the needs and desires of every last man, woman, and child on Earth? Do you think all the people of the world could fit within America's borders and be successfully fed, sheltered, and clothed?

No.

So if, for instance, the world was ending and the only safe place on the planet was the United States, who would we choose to save? Who do we choose to let in through our borders?

Because even America, with its vast resources, cannot solve the problems of the whole of the Earth. We are forced then, to protect what we have by making rational decisions. Most Americans take their lifestyles for granted and do not understand their freedoms.

Political correctness, in many ways, is causing some Americans to make emotional, irrational decisions.

But at the end of the day, you cannot please everyone. And if you try, you'll end up pleasing no one at all.

Venezuela

Do you know what's going on in Venezuela? The entire country is on the brink of economic collapse!

Supplies of food and medical care have slowly been decreasing since 2013 and are now at dangerously low levels, causing wide spread shortages. Inflation is expected to top 700 percent in 2017 alone.[8]

All of this is due to the massive devaluation of the Venezuelan currency (bolivar). In 2003, to prevent money from leaving the country after an oil strike, Hugo Chavez, the president at the time, implemented several currency controls. Since then, the bolivar has devalued by more than 99 percent, making long-term capital planning a nightmare. Small businesses cannot grow, and because of the high level of inflation, consumers cannot buy.[9]

The current administration, instead of lifting the regulations preventing economic growth, has tightened its reins, making the problem worse.

It's gotten so bad that amid a bread shortage, the Venezuelan government seized bakeries and detained bakers, claiming that the bakeries were trying to destabilize the country by price-gouging.

But the real problem was that Venezuela wasn't importing enough wheat needed to make bread. Those bakers were arrested for charging too much for bread, but the high price they were charging reflected the high cost of wheat. They were simply trying to run a business with a reasonable enough profit to stay in business.[10]

Without a profit, a baker would have no reason nor motivation to bake the bread to sell. Making a profit ensures bakers keep baking. Taking away a person's incentive to be a baker leads to no bakers. They weren't price-gouging; they were reacting internally to the high price of their supplies to ensure their own survival.

Excessive restrictions and regulations only hurt and stifle the working class. Capitalism, entrepreneurship, and free markets promote true, economic growth. The U.S. Constitution protects our rights as Americans. What happened in Venezuela cannot happen here as long as we hold true to the laws we have which safeguard economic freedom.

I have a client from Venezuela who was in the fruit extract oil export business, based in the U.S. He described this beautiful house that he has on a high cliff overlooking the ocean in Venezuela and how he had designed it with the most beautiful furnishings because it was to be his retirement dream home.

"Was?" I asked.

Was, he said because he used to rent it out while he conducted his business all over the U.S. He planned for it to be his retirement home.

But, he said, the government ruined that. He can no longer rent it out because the government changed the laws, making it impossible to evict a renter that does not pay.

And, because of the mess of the country, its property value, if he were to sell, is next to nothing.

So, he is now stuck with a house that he has to pay someone to visit once per week to keep it clean and appearing 'occupied' to ensure that no one breaks in. But he cannot rent it, sell it, or live in it because of the shortages and unrest in the country.

To me, this is a direct result of the socialist policies of the late President Hugo Chavez and his successor, Nicolas Maduro, after their United Socialist Party's 18 years in power. In fact, since about 95 percent of Venezuela's export revenues come from oil, while oil prices were high, Venezuela was able to give almost one million poor Venezuelans houses. But once oil prices dropped and left the government without a majority of their former revenue, they had to curtail many of their generous social programs, leading to shortages and civil unrest.[11] This points to one basic fundamental concept: with the exception of the military, the government is the net creator of nothing. It is simply a transferor of resources from where they currently exist to where the government wants them to be. If America is to remain the land of opportunity we discussed in the last chapter, we should keep this perspective on government at the forefront.

Protect the Poor

I know that a lot of you likely happily give generously of what you have to charity and to help those less fortunate. Most of us want to help those in need... but do you want to give them immediate relief or would you rather help create lasting change? Do you want to give them a fish or do you want to teach them how to fish for themselves?

Abraham Lincoln is credited with speaking on the difference between giving and empowering. He is attributed with saying:

> *You cannot bring about prosperity by discouraging thrift.*
> *You cannot strengthen the weak by weakening the strong.*
> *You cannot help little men by tearing down big men.*
> *You cannot lift the wage earner by pulling down the*
> *wage payer.*
> *You cannot help the poor by destroying the rich.*
> *You cannot establish sound security on borrowed money.*
> *You cannot further the brotherhood of man by inciting*
> *class hatred.*
> *You cannot build character and courage by destroying men's*
> *initiative and independence.*
> *And you cannot help men permanently by doing for them*
> *what they can and should do for themselves.*[12]

A lot of people are misguided in their approach to caring for those less fortunate, but research shows us that the best way to truly help the poor is through the use of free markets. A free market is defined as:

> "An economic system in which prices and wages
> are determined by unrestricted competition between
> businesses, without government regulation or fear
> of monopolies."[13]

In free markets, economic growth flourishes, benefiting both the working class and the poor. Free markets inspire hard work because they promote and reward those who work and achieve. Hand-outs only hold back our working class and make the poor dependent on the government.[14]

Even our founding fathers knew the biggest financial proponent for the poor and middle class was the free market system. That's partly why they wrote so many protections around free markets in the U.S. Constitution.

Universal Basic Income

When it comes to helping the poor and working class, we are seeing the reintroduction of an old idea again around the world. Some countries in Europe are already testing it out, and there is serious talk about it here in the U.S. It is the idea of a Universal Basic Income (UBI), paid to the people via their government.[15]

Mark Zuckerberg, the CEO of Facebook, is one proponent of the concept, arguing that a UBI would allow people to take risks and try new things because their basic living costs would be covered. He's basically saying that progress shouldn't be measured by economics but by meaningful experiences. He claims a UBI would be a "new social contract for our generation."[16]

When you are a billionaire 60 times over from your capitalistic, college-era invention, that might be a pretty easy thing to say.

The problem with a UBI, however, is that if everyone is given the same amount of money, every year, then the price of everything will simply rise proportionally. This is the economic concept of the 'invisible hand'. Giving everyone the same amount of money is essentially the equivalent of giving everyone nothing. It's totally ineffective economically.

Bono Gets It

Capitalism, entrepreneurship, and free markets are the best way to help the poor and working classes.

I am sure that you have heard of the band U2. From Ireland, they formed in 1976[17] and are still one of the most popular bands in the world.

The band's lead singer, Bono, is especially charismatic. He's a humanitarian and has been advocating for years for increased government aid for the world's poorest countries.

Bono, like many Americans, once believed that government aid was the best way to help the poorest people of the world. He probably didn't initially understand economics or how to create long-term, sustainable growth for those communities.

But Bono has since changed his tune. At a speech he gave at Georgetown University, he said, "Aid is just a stop-gap. Commerce, entrepreneurial capitalism, takes more people out of poverty than aid."[18]

Bono figured it out. He has spent the better part of his life searching for ways to help the less fortunate. And what is the answer all his searching has led to? Capitalism, entrepreneurship, and free markets.

It All Goes Back to Economics

Economics is the market equalizer of scarcity which exists in all things except, perhaps, the air we breathe. There are even studies on how water is, and will continue to be, the newest and scarcest commodity on Earth.

America's use of economics and the laws protecting those economics are unique. These laws help differentiate between the concepts of what is fair and what is equal. The two may sound like similar ideas, but they are vastly different, as we have seen.

Economics sets a fundamental equilibrium and creates borders around limited resources. But equilibrium doesn't mean fair, nor does it necessarily mean equal. When resources are distributed equally, it means that everyone is given the same share, as with the proposed UBI.

But is equal really fair? What if one person works harder than the other? What if one person doesn't work at all, even though they are capable of working? There is a limited amount of gold in the world. Should the person who mined it, the person who worked the hardest, and the person who put up the capital, each receive the same amount of gold as their neighbor who put forth no effort whatsoever towards the gold?

It reminds me of the childhood story by Margot Zemach and popularized by *Little Golden Books* called "The Little Red Hen." In the story, the little red hen finds a grain of wheat and asks for help from the other animals — a pig, a goat and a cat — to plant it, but they all decline.

Later, the red hen asks the other animals who will help harvest, thresh, and mill the wheat into flour, and then bake the flour into bread. But each time, and at every step, the other animals all refuse to help saying, "not I!"

Finally, the bread is ready and the little red hen asks which animal would help eat the bread and every animal happily volunteers. But having done all the work to make the bread herself, the little red hen replies, "No, I will eat it all by myself."

This childhood story can be summed up by the Bible verse *2 Thessalonians 3:10*, "…if any would not work, neither should he eat."

Distributing things equally is not just unfair, it really is not possible. Since the beginning of time, governments around the world have tried to do this — to create societies built on equality — but they have all failed. Socialism and communism, though they might sound good in theory, simply do not work in practice.

Capitalist China?

Even communist China has migrated to a quasi-privatized form of communism with two stages of large economic reforms beginning in 1978.

When agriculture was decollectivized, the country was opened to foreign investment and entrepreneurs were given permission to start businesses, with China retaining majority control.

In the second stage during the late 80s and 90s, China privatized much state-owned industry and lifted price controls, regulations, and protectionist policies. By 2005, as much as 70 percent of China's GDP was generated by the private sector.

However, there have been some government reversals since 2005, heavily regulating and controlling the economy like before the economic reforms.[19] And, the country's robust growth over the last decade has been largely artificially created through the government's vast infrastructure and development projects: the ghost cities.

China's Ghost Cities

There is an episode of 60-Minutes called "China's Real Estate Bubble" which explains how the country has been building several million-person "ghost" cities. These cities they have built are big enough to hold one million people and were (and still mostly are) completely empty. They built bridges, roads, malls, apartment and condominium buildings, and single-family homes. The demand for the necessary building materials, like steel and concrete, to build these cities was massive. This industrialization and real-estate "growth" was artificially sustaining China's economy with a GDP of about 8 percent. There are around 71 of these mostly empty one-million-person ghost cities which China believes will become populated by their population eventually relocating from rural areas to these urbanized cities that have sat waiting for them.[21]

Venezuela's government-funded social programs collapsed with the price declines in oil, so how long can China artificially support their own economy with these ghost infrastructure programs?

Furthermore, what will this mean for America when the ghost cities no longer artificially boost China's economy? A preview of that answer came in 2016, and it was not pretty.

At the start of 2016, we had the worst beginning year market performance in history, all thanks to China.[22]

As the new year began, Beijing announced the country's plans to move toward a consumer-based service economy and away from their hyper-inflated GDP growth through their decade-long industrialization.

At the time, China was the world's biggest consumer of commodities, so what do you think happened after this announcement was made? The price of crude oil and steel plummeted![23]

Their markets started to crash, and soon, markets around the world followed suit. It was a free fall; the worst start to the U.S. market in history.[24]

After the steep market volatility, Beijing reversed course and announced their renewed industrialized development focus to sustain their high GDP. Literally almost overnight, the price of oil and other commodities stabilized near their previous levels.

The majority of America woke up, bought their Starbucks, and went about their days, none the wiser as to why the markets were unstable at the beginning of the year or what had fixed the problem.

What most people didn't know was that the Chinese government injected one trillion dollars back into their economy in the first quarter of 2016. It was the *largest single-quarter government infusion of capital in the history of the world*. And it single-handedly stabilized the world's economy. Now that is scary.

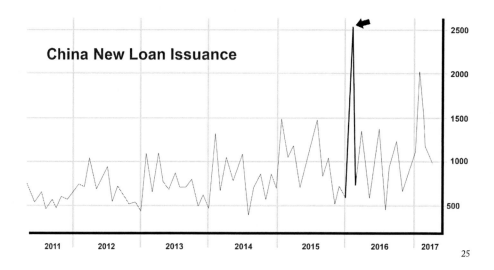

25

Consumer-Based Economies

For over a decade, China had sustained high demand for commodities in order to build their ghost cities.

Announcing that they were transitioning from their industrial building phase and into a service-based economy meant they would no longer be purchasing mass quantities of all the commodities needed to build massive cities, including crude oil, steel, copper, and so on.

It also meant that now the Chinese economy would need the support of its citizens in order to grow. It meant the Chinese people needed to start buying things, and they needed to start migrating from their rural neighborhoods into those ghost cities.

But even though China has 1.4 billion people,[26] their citizens only had an average per capita disposable income of $3,469 in 2016.[27] This is compared to 320 million Americans[28] who had $43,536 in per capita disposable annual income[29] that same year. Now you see the problem.

How can China transition to a consumer-service based economy when their citizens have such a small disposal income? They have a lot less money to spend than the average American — where America has definitely become a service-based economy.

It seems impossible to move to a consumer-based economy when your gross disposable domestic income is less than $3,500 per person. Making a full transition to a consumer-based economy would have been incredibly problematic and the world saw that instantly. China had been inflating their growth rates artificially by building ghost cities, but as soon as they announced their decision to pull back on their created growth, the price for commodities went straight down and our market had its worst start in history.[30]

You can't fake the economics of real growth forever. Eventually, it will catch up with you.

Self-Reliance and Self-Determination

As we have gone through in this chapter and the last one, America is under attack today by political correctness and the infliction of elitism. We are preached at by celebrities, tech gurus, and numerous others, that striving for absolute equality is the noblest goal; that inequality of wealth and resources should be rectified with government redistribution and open borders. They ask, who are we to keep people out of our country and keep them from having the opportunities we have? We've been told that the government should even provide a universal basic income to every person just for being alive.

Yet, these are the very same people that have three separate levels of security for their own awards show within their own city. It seems quite easy, but rather disingenuous, to say what everyone else should do and what everyone else should tolerate when you are not doing it yourself.

This is why Bono of U2 deserves genuine respect. Because he actually traveled the globe for years, actively trying to make a difference, and has seen for himself that enabling people to better their own life is far superior than any government program or handout.

The bottom line is, we cannot pretend that America has all the resources required to solve the entire world's problems. As great of a country as we are, it remains a fact that we, too, have finite resources and could not accept the whole of the Earth's population into our lands.

Once you accept that there is just not enough for everyone, you have to create perimeters and laws that determine who is allowed to come and remain within those perimeters. It is just that simple and no amount of political correctness can change this.

All of this comes down to the basic reality that you must take individual ownership of your life. You must take control. What is your life going to mean? What are you going to become? You cannot be apathetic.

And you surely cannot rely on the government to take care of you. Like I've stated before, everyone is born with the innate desire to make something of themselves.

As we have seen, even China has modernized their communism into a regime with quasi-privatized companies as a labor incentive. Chinese citizens are now incentivized to work harder so they can make more money.

Complete government ownership fails every time. Why? Because of that innate human desire to make something of yourself. Humans have a desire to accomplish. Take away the hard-earned rewards for making something of yourself and you extinguish that innate desire; people become unmotivated and apathetic.

Luckily for Americans, our Constitution was written to promote that desire, not hinder it.

Programs designed to take care of people do the exact opposite. Instead of taking personal responsibility for their financial security, they learn to depend solely upon those programs.

Social Security is a perfect example of that problem. The program was designed to keep people just above poverty and to supplement other retirement vehicles. But now, millions and millions of Americans depend on Social Security as their only means of survival. Is that the kind of lifestyle you want?

Our system advocates self-reliance and self-determination, making it the best system in the world. We were all born with a hunger to accomplish more and luckily for us, our founding documents were written to promote that.

But if America allows these elitist ideals to take root and deconstruct everything that makes America unique and special, what control will you have over your own destiny and the life you are able to create then? The need to protect everything that's great about the United States has never been more critical. Understanding the economics of scarcity, finite resources are always pitted against unlimited needs and demands, we can better appreciate our need for the law, our status as Americans, and our opportunity to craft our own destiny.

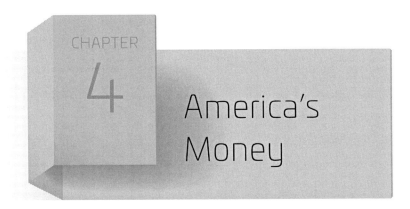

CHAPTER

4

America's Money

How Did We Get Here?

We have talked about economics, the law, and American exceptionalism, and how these make up the foundation of our understanding and our ability to create wealth in America.

Now we turn to money and our background of money in America. We start with a question. At our core do we, America, have an understanding of what we have been doing for the last 70-plus years?

As a nation, we enjoy and have come to expect a standard of living that we cannot and do not support through our own annual economic productivity.

In reality, we are living off the future productivity of our heirs, borrowing against their future successes for our present day, for a standard of living that we do not earn and cannot sustain.

How did we get here? How did we ever allow our country to rack up over $20 trillion dollars in debt?

Our Faith in Paper Money

This book is all about taking control, and many of you believe that if you own gold, you are taking control of your financial future.

Gold is a tangible asset set apart from all other commodities because of its unique characteristics. It is unique in that, while other commodities can be consumed and will disappear, it cannot be consumed, nor can it disappear. Instead, it gets accumulated.

The first connotation of gold is that of money. Many Americans believe that even if the economy collapses, as long as they have gold hidden underneath their floorboards, they'll be fine.

But many of these same Americans don't know the history of gold in our country. They don't know that the gold bars they're investing in can and have been captured by the government, at any moment.

Gold has been used as a form of currency since 550 B.C.[31]

Mercantilism was challenged by Adam Smith's "The Wealth of Nations,"[32] which, in large part, became the treatise of our New World and the birth of America Capitalism. Paper money, exchangeable for gold, became a necessary stand-in because heavy gold was an impractical medium of exchange. Settlers went West to seek their fortunes in gold. Changes in the exchange rate of paper dollars to gold partially led to the creation of the Federal Reserve in 1913.[33]

The stock market and economic crashes of the Great Depression, starting in 1929, collapsed our faith in paper money and caused multiple bank runs, including on the Federal Reserve Bank of New York in 1933. President Franklin D. Roosevelt closed the banks in March of 1933 and issued Executive Order #6102, requiring all persons to "deliver on or before May 1, 1933, all gold coin, gold bullion, and gold certificates" to the Federal Reserve in exchange for $20.67 paper dollars per ounce.[34]

On June 5, 1933, Congress nullified the right of creditors to demand loan repayments in gold.[35] The president's executive order requiring privately held gold be turned in to the federal reserve in exchange for paper money, along with the Gold Reserve Act of 1934 – which fixed the price of gold at $35 dollars per ounce and led many other nations to transfer their gold to America[36] – made the United States the sole country with the largest gold reserves in the world, a status it retains to this day.[37]

The World's De Facto Currency

Owning gold, except a de minimis amount, remained illegal for 40 years from 1933 through 1974, when President Ford signed a bill, PL 93-373, to again legalize private ownership of gold coins, bars, and certificates.[38]

World War II ended the Great Depression,[39] but the world's costs and reserves required for the expansive war effort led countries to mostly abandon their gold standards and leverage the use of debt financing.[40]

The 1944 Bretton Woods Agreement set the exchange value of worldwide currencies in terms of gold, and gold was set to exchange at $35 U.S. dollars per ounce.[41] And with the U.S. holding the world's largest gold reserves, most countries used dollars for their reserves since dollars were convertible into gold at a fixed rate. This led countries to ultimately peg their currency to the dollar instead, with central banks maintaining fixed exchange rates between their currency and the dollar via foreign exchange markets.[42]

This eliminated the need for most countries to exchange their currency for gold, making the dollar the world's de facto reserve currency.[43]

A Final Nail in the Gold Standard Coffin

President Nixon put the final nail in the gold standard coffin when he prevented the Federal Reserve from exchanging dollars for gold in 1971.[44] The U.S. government reset the price of gold in dollars per ounce, but then completely disassociated the dollar from gold altogether in 1976.[45]

When the dollar, then soundly established as the world's reserve currency, was decoupled from gold, *economic growth the world over was no longer pinned to a finite asset.*

And it soared... along with our national debt. Printing dollars and selling dollars to our worldwide neighbors, untethered to gold, brought additional prosperity to America.

Safety in Gold Accumulation

Now that gold is once again legal to own, I know many Americans who believe accumulating the precious metal is a great alternative strategy for building wealth. They *really* believe in the economic power of gold.

Don't get me wrong, I am a fan of gold, too, but history has a sneaky way of repeating itself. In 1933, with the stroke of his pen, President Roosevelt implemented an executive order that forced Americans to surrender their gold to the U.S. Government in exchange for paper currency. This could just as easily happen again for the sake of national security, economic stabilization, or whatever reason the president attributes it to at that point in history.

Sadly, many, if not most of America, never knew or have forgotten this part of our history. Knowledge really is power. The more you know, the less likely you are to be caught off guard. You might think you're taking control by owning tangible, valuable assets like gold but how much control do you really have, especially with 1933 as an example?

America, and America Alone

America, as the world's reserve currency, has enjoyed the freedom to print dollars at will; dollars that have been bought up out of necessity for the international exchanges between countries that did not want each other's domestic currencies while trading amongst themselves.

And so, since the 1940s, America has enjoyed some largess of life that has not been earned based solely on domestic economic productivity.

If President Roosevelt hadn't signed that infamous executive order in 1933, and if the government hadn't accumulated the largest reserve of gold in the world, the U.S. dollar might never have become the world's reserve currency in 1944. That executive order and the Gold Reserve Act of 1934 gave the dollar strength and massive economic power. It enabled the American lifestyle we still take advantage of to this day. But, America would not have our unique position in the world were it not for this history.

And this history that gave us great wealth also influenced us to live well outside our means. We have been living off our future heirs since the U.S. dollar became a world reserve currency.

Golden Security – Not So Much

Gold isn't the end all, be all. Gold doesn't really allow you to take control. Not really. It's just as volatile as any other asset. Its worth goes up and goes down. It doesn't give you any cash flow, nor does it give you any kind of compounded rate of return, beyond its value increasing against the dollar. These truths, coupled with the fact that the government could take it away at any time, make relying on gold a really poor retirement strategy.

But could there come a day when the world no longer needs the U.S. dollar?

Many have never contemplated a world operating outside of the dollar, while others ignore the alarm bells ringing all around us. These alarms are real and deafening, and include the unprecedented, rapid development of bilateral trade in domestic currencies between the world's largest economies, including China and Japan, China and Russia, and BRICS — Brazil, Russia, India, China and South Africa — among others.

A New World Reserve Currency?

Both the United Nations and the IMF (International Monetary Fund) have pushed for a new world reserve currency for years and have developed an alternative: Special Drawing Rights (SDRs). SDRs represent a basket of five currencies: the euro, the Japanese yen, the British pound sterling, the U.S. dollar, and now the Chinese yuan (also known as the renminbi).[46]

SDRs were created in 1969 but were of little utility until they recently proved a crucial player in providing liquidity to the world economy during the global financial crisis in 2009.

However, given recent, unparalleled financial events, including first-time-ever-in-history negative interest rates, the Brexit vote, and China's currency devaluations, among others, the world is flocking back to the perceived safety of the dollar in droves.

Ironically, this could backfire on the U.S. by making China's financial position untenable.[47] China would have few options, leading them to likely either severely devalue their currency or call for the removal of the dollar as the sole reserve currency,[48] either of which would be devastating.[49]

In addition to this, the rise of cryptocurrencies like Bitcoin, which are by design outside the control of centralized governments, are but another way around the dollar in the foreseeable future, especially as they are rapidly becoming accepted as legal tender in many countries across the globe.

American Arrogance?

Has America taken for granted its special status as the owner of the world's reserve currency? Do we live as though we expect this special status to last indefinitely? And how long can any country, especially the leader of the world, spend more than it takes in by over $500 billion per year?[50]

The United States' special status as the sole world reserve currency has intoxicated its citizens with an unsustainable lifestyle, one that could not be possible if not for the other nations of the world being involuntarily tethered to the dollar in order to transact their international business.

Never have we been so close to that becoming a model of the past. What does America look like then? What will our country look like when the world has the ability to turn its back on the almighty dollar? What effect will that have on our markets?

Whether it happens in two days, 20 years, or not at all, even the idea of a new currency creates volatility within the market.

How can it not?

The dollar is tied to governments and economies around the world. When faith in it starts to wane, those economies and those countries will naturally suffer.

Currency devaluation means stock devaluation, too.

The world's belief in the power of the U.S. dollar is on the decline. The need to take control of your personal finances by making the right wealth building choices is more crucial than it ever has been, and gold alone cannot be the singular solution.

PART

2

WHY
WE
AREN'T
WHERE
WE
SHOULD
BE

5

The Way America Retires Now

Just Sign on the Dotted Line

During the last two years of my undergraduate finance program, I worked part-time in commercial lending at Bank of America (then NationsBank). Before I graduated, I secured a full-time job with Price Waterhouse LLP.

On my first day, I went through an on-boarding process with Human Resources. I was given a packet of paperwork to review and complete, and right behind my offer letter was a pre-populated form designed to enroll me in the company's 401(k) plan.

All I had to do was check the box indicating the level of withholding I wanted and sign on the dotted line. It was that easy.

And that really sums up how America retires today: through pre-tax defined contribution plans. For most of you, that means a 401(k), while for others, it could mean the 403(b), the 457, the TSP, the IRA, SIMPLE, or the SEP.

Regardless of the type, these pre-tax defined contribution plans have become the default retirement method in America. But how did we get here?

Why Weren't We Taught How to Build Wealth?

The day you started your first real job of your career, do you remember what you knew about retiring? You were probably in your early 20s and most likely didn't give a thought to your last day of working or to what retirement would look like for you. Most people do not know anything about retirement when they are just starting their careers.

Let's be honest, who even cares about retiring when you are just starting your first real job? Unless you were among the lucky few whose family discussed deeper, long-term life and financial topics, you probably didn't know anything about retirement. Most of us haven't been taught anything about finance or retirement, let alone the best method of building wealth. It really is quite ironic given that America is the "Land of Opportunity" and many argue it has been the leader of the free world since the end of World War II.

So, shouldn't our country's retirement mechanisms be the best in the world? Shouldn't we lead the way in how the world retires?

We should have gone to the mathematical and statistical experts at MIT, or even the London School of Economics, to devise a retirement methodology that would, to the best extent possible, be recession proof, inflation proof, and tax-advantaged.

But, we did not. That never happened.

Sadly, in fact, our main retirement vehicle happened *by accident.*

Created by Accident

Believe it or not, the development of America's main method of saving for retirement, the 401(k), happened by accident.

It started as a corporate tax dodge for highly compensated executives and became a permanent part of the IRC (Internal Revenue Code) with the Revenue Act of 1978.

Some reports reveal that the law firm for Hughes Aircraft Corporation recommended they start to amend their savings plan to utilize the new 401(k) provision as early as 1978, but at first, this new tax provision was mostly ignored. Most employers had savings plans that allowed employees to put after-tax money in, which was then matched by the employer.[51]

But in September 1979, all that changed.

Ted Banna, a benefits consultant who worked for a small firm in Philadelphia, The Johnson Companies, needed to come up with a way for a bank client to replace their cash bonuses with a tax-deferred profit sharing plan instead, one that employees wouldn't be able to access until they left the bank's employment. Banna had the idea to use the new 401(k) provision to allow employees to defer their cash bonus, pre-tax, with a corporate match.[52]

The bank client decided not to use the plan Banna developed because they didn't want to implement something never used before. But that didn't change the fact that *many* employers were looking for new ways to offer employee benefits and retirement plans. New funding reserve requirements had been mandated under ERISA, the Employee Retirement Income Security Act, to prevent employers from underfunding their employees' pension plans. Companies were looking for alternatives to their defined benefit pension plans that, under the new law, now had to be much more heavily funded.[53]

The bank's refusal didn't stop Banna from pioneering the way for his new plan. He didn't think it was fair for 401(k) plans to only be offered to highly-paid corporate executives, but that they should be available to *everyone*.

Banna convinced his company to implement his newly designed inclusive plan, and The Johnson Companies was the first to implement the new 401(k) system, launching the 401(k) revolution.

Now, more than 35 years later, the 401(k) and its pre-tax defined contribution plan cousins are the most-used retirement vehicle in existence.[54]

Designed to Be a Tax Dodge, Not Stand-Alone Quality

Initially, the 401(k) was designed to be a tax dodge for high compensated employees who were already on a defined benefit pension plan. It was designed to be a bonus on top of an already established retirement plan. It was not designed nor meant to be an actual stand-alone, sole retirement plan. Even Banna recounts how his plan was just meant to replace annual cash bonuses rather than the employees' actual retirement plan.

But ironically, that's exactly what happened.

Because the 401(k) was originally designed only to act as a bonus on top of a pension plan, no one looked or analyzed it as a *replacement retirement vehicle*. Consequently, no one did any due diligence, no one ran any statistical analysis, or performance simulations to verify and ensure the long-term practicality of a 401(k) as a retirement vehicle when it was first introduced.

Before we decided to change the way America retires, we should have calculated mathematical, statistical, and scientific probabilities to determine whether this plan would adequately provide for retirement. But you do not test and plan when things happen *by accident*.

Today, we use something called a **Monte Carlo Simulation**, which allows us to run approximately 5,000 simulations simultaneously. We can test the longevity of a portfolio against market highs and lows and inflation highs and lows. We can test against interest rate highs and lows. Based on the defined spend rate, number of years in distribution, and starting portfolio balance, we can run all of it, at the same time, to determine the mathematical, statistical probability of a portfolio running out of money during retirement.

But back in the early 1980s, no one used the tools at our disposal today to determine whether the 401(k) was a viable retirement option. Considering all of America's technological, economic, medicinal, and scientific advances, the fact that we didn't perform our due diligence before changing the way America retires is quite ridiculous.

Basically, we winged it. We used a program that was already in the tax code but designed for some other purpose. We ignored the original intent of the 401(k) and, without verifying whether it was viable, rolled it out to everyone as their main retirement option. Even Banna himself has publicly stated the plan was never intended to supplant or be used instead of a traditional retirement vehicle and regrets how it has been implemented and used.[55]

The Rise of the 401(k)

When the 401(k) was introduced to America, it changed the way most of us retire. As a whole, the rise of the 401(k) really led to the demise of the company pension.

Not sure what the difference is?

A 401(k) is a pre-tax, defined contribution plan. That means that the employee contributes pre-tax dollars into a company sponsored investment account. These accounts are typically tied to market performance and cannot be touched without a 10 percent tax penalty until age 59 1/2, with some exceptions. When withdrawals are made, those withdrawals are subject to taxes.

A pension is a defined benefit plan and is typically financed by the employer. It *guarantees* an individual a retirement payment when the employee retires. The size of the pension typically depends on length of service, seniority, and earned income.

One of the main differences between the two plans is that a 401(k) is managed by the employee and the pension is managed by the employer.[56]

In the 1960s and 70s, most Americans retired via corporate America's private pension system. As soon as the 401(k) was introduced, the percentage of workers covered by traditionally defined benefit pension plans started to decrease.

In fact, it's been declining, consistently, ever since. In just over two decades, private sector pension coverage fell by over half.[57] In 1975, 87 percent of qualified, private workforce employees were enrolled in a defined benefit pension plan. In 1998, that number dropped to just 12 percent.[58]

This data and those numbers represent the workforce as it was almost 20 years ago — and that is the most recent data reported. Based on the way pension enrollment was dropping in the late 90s, imagine what percentage of workers are enrolled in defined benefit pension plans now.

The Demise of the Pension

If you think about it, pensions are mostly a thing of the past. How many people do you know that currently have a pension? Of the companies that do still offer pension plans, many of them often offer lump sum buy-outs to reduce their long term cost exposure.

So, unless you know someone that worked for GM or other major American corporations for over 20+ years or the government — including those in the federal, state, and local levels, along with members of the military — you're probably coming up short. That's because pensions have been steadily declining since the mid-1980s.

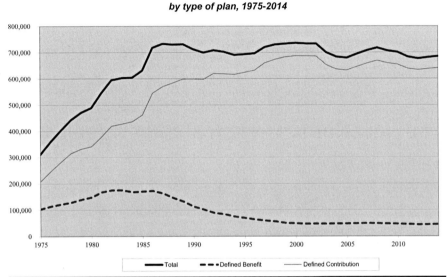

Number of Pension Plans
by type of plan, 1975-2014

NOTE: The methods used to develop the statistics in this report have changed over time. These changes are outlined in Appendices B through G.

NOTE: Excludes "one-participant plans."

SOURCE: Form 5500 filings with the U.S. Department of Labor.

https://www.dol.gov/sites/default/files/ebsa/researchers/statistics/retirement-bulletins/private-pension-plan-bulletin-historical-tables-and-graphs.pdf

A Terrible Substitute

Pensions are virtually disappearing, making way for the 401(k)'s total dominance as America's main retirement vehicle since the early 1980s. So what's the big deal?

Simply put, as a retirement strategy, pre-tax defined contribution plans like 401(k)s, 403(b)s, and so on *have utterly failed us.* They have turned out to be a terrible substitute for defined benefit pension plans.

Prominent economist Teresa Ghilarducci claims the 401(k) is a failed experiment. It has failed middle-class Americans because it was never designed with them in mind. In fact, the system was set-up to work against them.[59]

Over the years, economists, analysts, and mathematicians alike have criticized the 401(k) system as a means of retirement. But *why* are they failing?

I believe that 401(k)s are failing due to four main reasons: market volatility, emotional investing, the retirement savings gap, and tax policy. Each of these reasons deserve their own chapter, but let's take a quick look at each.

The New Normal – High Market Volatility

Market volatility is the first obvious reason the 401(k) is failing.

When it comes to the stock market, high volatility is the *New Normal.* Right now, the S&P 500 is up 281 percent since the low of the Great Recession on March 9, 2009.

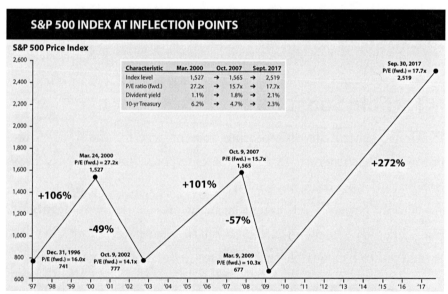

S&P 500 INDEX AT INFLECTION POINTS

S&P 500 Price Index

Characteristic	Mar. 2000		Oct. 2007		Sept. 2017
Index level	1,527	→	1,565	→	2,519
P/E ratio (fwd.)	27.2x	→	15.7x	→	17.7x
Divident yield	1.1%	→	1.8%	→	2.1%
10-yr Treasury	6.2%	→	4.7%	→	2.3%

Graph recreated from information provided by: Compustat, FactSet, Thomson Reuters, Federal Reserve, Standard & Poor's, J.P. Morgan Asset Management.
Dividend yield is calculated as consensus estimates of dividends for the next 12 months, divided by most recent price, as provided by Compustat.
Forward price to earnings ratio is a bottom-up calculation based on the most recent S&P 500 Index price, divided by consensus estimates for earnings in the next 12 months (NTM), and is provided by FactSet Market Aggregates. Returns are cumulative and based on S&P 500 Index price movement only, and do not include the reinvestment of dividends. Past performance is not indicative of future returns. Guide to the Markets - U.S. Data are as of September 30, 2017.

High volatility doesn't only mean intense market increases, but devastating market lows, as well. From 2000 through 2016, the S&P 500 total returns averaged only a 4.5 percent rate of return. This was due to the three consecutive years of losses in 2000, 2001, and 2002 during the bursting of the "dot com" bubble, and the Great Recession of 2007-2009, with a 57 percent drop from the October 2007 peak to the March 2009 trough. The S&P 500 has only had three consecutive years of losses three times in our history: during the Great Depression, during World War II, and during the technology bubble at the turn of the millennium.

Our *New Normal*, since the 90s, is extreme volatility – uncharacteristically high highs followed by extraordinary low lows. These vast changes have a severe impact our wealth. Lost money is a real opportunity cost: for every dollar you lose, it's a dollar that's also no longer earning interest.

Market guys will tell you to buy and hold through volatile times, that investing is a long-term strategy, and that your account will recover and grow back. But is that true?

No, not really. Yes, if you hold long enough, your account value will eventually return to its former heights, but that is a function of your reduced balance continuing to grow and any additional funds you continue to invest. During the Great Recession, it took the S&P 500 over four years to completely return to its pre-crash levels – keep in mind that if you want to replicate this recovery in your own portfolio, you must take NO portfolio withdrawals during that same time period.

This Buy and Hold strategy reminds me of a personal example. The year of my 15th wedding anniversary, my husband and I decided to celebrate by going out of the country on our first scuba diving trip since our children were born. Since it had literally been 10 years since our last dive, we decided to take a PADI refresher course.

All was good until I got home and saw my engagement ring on my hand with four empty prongs and no diamond.

I was on the radio the next day and was still so upset that I ended up telling my audience what had happened.

All of a sudden, it hit me! This was a perfect example of the Buy and Hold strategy most market guys espouse. Yes, my husband will go out and replace my lost diamond ring, and I will, once more, have a diamond on my hand.

But that does not mean that I did not LOSE my original diamond! No, my original diamond was a true loss and getting a new one will not change that fact. Much the same as when your investment grows again, you have still lost the value you had before the downturn — you still had a loss, you just have new growth that masks the fact that you did have a true loss. To see this even more clearly, if you had avoided that loss and still received the growth that followed, your account value would be much larger than it is when you lose and then grow back – it would be like me having two diamonds instead of one. Now, that sounds a lot better.

How will these losses to your retirement impact your overall lifetime wealth building strategy? Well, a $100,000 loss at age 55 is the equivalent of $168,948 at a retirement age of 66, assuming that $100,000 grew at 6 percent per year. If the person who lost the $100,000 dies at age 88, the real dollars lost in wealth in that person's lifetime is $608,810, assuming the $100,000 lost would have grown an average of 6 percent over the 31 year period.

	TRUE COST OF CAPITAL LOSS	TRUE COST OF CAPITAL LOSS OVER LIFETIME
AGE WHEN MONEY WAS LOST	57	57
RETIREMENT AGE	66	88
YEARS LOST	9	31
ESTIMATED GROWTH	6%	6%
TOTAL COST OF CAPITAL LOSS	$168,948	$608,810

So, when the market is up, you win, but when it's down, you really do lose.

Emotionally Connected to Our Money

I was meeting with a potential client for the second time to go through and review the performance of his existing portfolio. I pointed out a position that was clearly underperforming and said that this would be a good candidate to sell quickly. The potential client responded, "I know, I know… but last week it was 50 cents higher, and I just want to wait for it to get back up to that level again before I sell it."

I saw, exemplified in this client, what the whole of America does when the market begins its down cycle. Even though conventional wisdom is to buy low and sell high, no one wants to sell at the highs. Stock owners see the market doing well, think it will continue to trend upwards, and don't want to miss out on even more potential additional growth should they sell now.

As a result, they wind up missing their best window through which to sell while the market is high. Then, just like this prospective client, when the market begins to drop, they remember its previous high and just want to get it back to that before they sell. Much like the Vegas gambler who just wants to make his lost money back and ends up losing a lot more, this common destructive market strategy becomes a vicious cycle.

This is what we in the financial business call **emotional investing**. Wisdom tells us to buy low and sell high, but historically, for emotional reasons, because it is our money, we do just the opposite.

In fact, Americans often buy at the top of the market, because they feel like it is proof that stocks are doing well so it must be a good decision to buy in.

But buying in at a high means you are counting on an even higher high in order to make your investment worthwhile. And instead of buying in when the market is low, many tend to think it means that something is wrong with the market or the overall economy, so they wait for a recovery before buying in – thus missing out on leveraging a market on sale. This only ensures that we buy at a more expensive price instead of simply buying at the low like we are supposed to do.

Emotionally, we are all naturally led to make the exact opposite investment decisions than we should logically be making. We make these irrational decisions, contrary to what we know we should do, because it is our money and we are emotionally connected to it.

It is for this same reason that 401(k)s fail. When it's *our* money, something we worked *hard* for, we cannot help but get emotional and make irrational decisions.

When the market is doing well, people want to invest. They decide to buy, thinking the market will continue to go up.

But when the market dips, at first those same people hold on, hoping to recoup their losses. Eventually, the market gets so low that they panic and end up selling everything because they simply cannot afford to lose another penny.

Emotional investing is capable of single-handedly ruining your financial future. The effects of emotional investing are clear when you compare the average investor's returns over the last 10, 20, and 30 years to what the market has done over the same time periods. Over the 10 year period from 2003-2013, investors with a blend of fixed income mutual funds and equities, on average, saw a return of just 2.6 percent. Over 20- and 30-year annualized periods, the return rate dropped to a measly 2.5 percent and 1.9 percent respectively, but the market itself over that same period had returns of over 7 percent.[62]

The average investor's growth rates are terrible, and the difference between these and market returns are in large part due to emotional investing. No wonder most Americans are behind when it comes to investing and building wealth!

Summing it up, emotionally, we buy high because we react to the current success of the market. We sell low because we get to a point that we cannot afford to lose any more. Then we take risks and gamble, hoping we'll get our money back. According to the average investor's long-term growth rates, it's obvious that the risks aren't paying off.

We Aren't Saving Enough

Pre-tax defined contribution plans are failing because people simply aren't saving nearly enough. This lack of savings is called the **Retirement Savings Gap** (RSG).

Pensions were designed, controlled, and funded by the employer. Contributing enough to fund the pension was the responsibility of the employer. But 401(k)s were designed to be controlled by the individual contributor... and that's part of the problem.

In 2016, of the American families that are actually contributing to a 401(k) plan, they had an average of $92,500 saved in 401(k)s or IRAs. But 15 years earlier, in 2001, the average saved was $91,243. That's a difference of just over $1,000 for a 15-year period.[63]

Considering what we know about the decline of company sponsored pensions, these balances are hardly enough as a stand-alone vehicle expected to provide a comfortable retirement.[64] And what is of even greater concern is that Vanguard reports that for the same period, the median 401(k) balance is $26,405, which means that half of all 401(k) accounts have $26,405 or less.[65]

Remember, the $92,500 is the *average* amount saved. It accounts for the people who have millions upon millions saved as well as the people who have almost nothing saved at all. To break it down specifically, 10 percent of us have more than $274,000 saved, and the bottom 50 percent of us have next to nothing saved for retirement.[66]

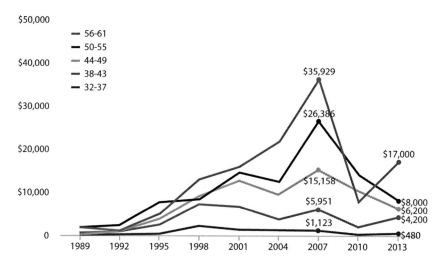

Most families-even those approaching retirement-have little or no retirement savings

Median retirement account savings of families by age,
1989-2013 (2013 dollars)

Note: Scale changed for visibility. Retirement account savings include 40 (k)s, IRAs, and Keogh plans.
Graph recreated from information provided by: EPI analysis of Survey of Consumer Finance data, 2013.

Why is this happening?

Pensions spoiled Americans regarding their individual responsibility towards their retirement. We were working, we were getting paid, and our employers were taking care of what needed to be done to provide us with guaranteed retirement income. They took the risks, and they made the decisions. We didn't have to do anything ourselves.

But the 401(k) revolution changed all that. Today, we have to make the decisions as individuals. We assumed the risk without anyone ever telling the average American what needed to be saved per year to achieve retirement security and success. No one told us what needed to be saved to successfully replicate what we would have received through a pension.

We didn't know how to properly save to reach retirement goals. We didn't know that we really needed to be saving at least 25 percent of what we earn for at least 30 years.

Fidelity has two benchmarks on how much someone utilizing a 401(k) should have in their account to be ready for retirement. By the time you're 30, you should have saved the equivalent of half of your annual salary; by age 40, that of twice your annual salary; by age 50, four times your salary; by age 60, six times; and by age 67, eight times. If you reach 67 years old and are making $75,000 per year, you should have $600,000 saved.

But these figures are much, much less than what the tried-and-true old-school 80 percent rule says you should have saved by retirement. The 80 percent rule says to save as much as you would need to get paid 80 percent of your salary for about 20 years. That would require about $1.2 million for that same person making $75,000, if you don't factor inflation into the calculations. Inflation would shoot that number up to between $1.5 million and $1.8 million.[67]

Now, our retirement dreams are in jeopardy... all because of this pesky 401(k).

Tax Problem

The 401(k) is a pre-tax plan, which means that you will pay ordinary income tax for the rest of your life during your retirement. This issue is so large that it requires its own chapter, so let's put a pin in that for now.

Arming Yourself with Knowledge

The 401(k) does not offer much promise for the financial future of most Americans, yet it is the most predominant retirement vehicle in existence. If your company offers any kind of retirement plan, chances are, it's a 401(k).

That's why arming yourself with this knowledge is so important. Understanding pre-tax defined contribution plans and all their shortcomings is the first step toward creating Wealth Unbroken.

This is what my practice does day in and day out, and it is what I am incredibly passionate about.

The next chapter is going to take a deep dive into the details of market volatility, a major wealth killer.

6 Fundamental Flaw #1 – Volatility

My Son's Trike

I have always been an athletic person; I've done gymnastics, dance, and cheerleading throughout my life. This has naturally translated into me being an active mom playing with my children. One Sunday afternoon in early October when I was 42 years old, I got my son's tricycle out to play around with my kids, as I had done many times before. Only this time was different. This time I decided to ride my son's tricycle down a small hill — or what I thought was small at the time. Rolling down that hill, I discovered *too late* that I had grossly miscalculated and felt like a steam engine about to race off its tracks. I had to decide whether to stay going out-of-control downhill or to turn into the grass and hope for a gentle landing. It was a no-brainer and in a split second, I made a hard-right straight into the grass. The dense grass stopped the trike instantly — it stopped, I did not. I flew off over the toy and straight into the grass, shoulder first! My first thought was that I was paralyzed. I immediately tried to move my legs, which thankfully moved. I shouted out to my family who were now running quickly towards me, "I'm okay, I'm okay, but don't touch me, DO NOT TOUCH ME!" The pain hit hard. Splitting pain ripped through me. I had broken my right clavicle — my first and only time breaking a bone. I'm now mended with a titanium rod in place, but the valuable lesson I learned that day has stayed with me and can, of course, be translated to finance. The toys you use, much like the financial tools you use, change with time. Also, riding your child's kid-sized tricycle is a horrible idea, especially after 40!

Mount Everest

When thinking of a person's financial lifecycle, I picture Mount Everest.

If you're a mountain climber, you know that there are three clear legs to the journey: the ascent, the summit, and the descent.

The ascent is the climb and the hard work. It's the blood, sweat, and tears.

The summit is the culmination of that hard work, the accomplishment, where you firmly plant your flag as a rite of passage.

And the descent — which one would think would be the easy part, just the climb down — is the rumination of the accomplishment, the enjoyment.

But, of all the deaths that have occurred on Mount Everest, over 80 percent have occurred upon descent in an area called the "death zone." This death zone is extremely devoid of oxygen. Arriving at the summit and descending later in the day, along with excessive fatigue, are all components most associated with this statistic. These climbers had enough juice to get up to the top, but not enough to get back down to the bottom.

Our financial life cycle follows this same trajectory, and retirement is filled with the same hidden dangers as descending Mt. Everest. Climbing a mountain is really a near perfect analogy of our financial life.

Ascent: The long, uphill battle of wealth accumulation. It is working, acquiring, saving and building for your future self in retirement and your family's legacy, working towards a major lifetime milestone.

Summit: That special moment when your entire adult life, as you have known it, changes because you have reached the peak, ending the accumulation phase of life, and are about to begin the second phase of your financial life cycle. As you transition from exchanging your time and energy to earn income and build wealth to placing that accumulated wealth in your place to now work for you, you breathe a sigh of relief: you've reached Retirement. Your accumulated wealth now steps in and takes over, working for you in your place, for the rest of your life.

Descent: The second phase of our financial life cycle after reaching Retirement is the distribution phase — where we must put our exit strategy to work for us — navigating and managing our wealth to ensure that we maintain our lifestyle and will not outlive our money during our retirement years.

Just like Everest, most Americans fail, financially, upon the descent. They have not properly developed a sustainable exit strategy, a distribution strategy that will see them through their retirement years. Most are unprepared to maintain their lifestyle throughout retirement and will not reach the end like they wish to. Frankly, most Americans are ill-prepared for retirement.

The Way We Used to Retire

Retiring today is not what it used to be... we are in a *New Normal* of major market volatility. And volatility is our new nemesis.

But what happened to the way we used to retire?

Before the 80s, most retirees used to prepare for retirement in just one way: they worked for a company for almost their entire career and knew they would have both a company pension, their accumulated savings, and Social Security to maintain their retirement lifestyle.

After the early 80s and the wide reception and implementation of the 401(k), Americans traded their company-funded pension for the do-it-yourself pre-tax 401(k).

Then, as they retired, they would move their savings out of the market into a fixed, guaranteed vehicle (like a Certificate of Deposit (CD) at a bank with 6 to 7 percent returns) that had no risk of principal loss. Combined with Social Security, their pension or their 401(k), and their savings, they were basically set for the rest of their lives.

S&P 500 Bull Markets Since WWII

	Months it lasted	Total % gain
10/1990-03/2000	113	417
3/2009-unknown	96	249
6/1949-8/1956	86	267
10/1974-11/1980	74	126
08/1982-08/1987	60	229
10/2002-10/2007	60	101
10/1957-12/1961	50	86
5/1962-2/1966	44	80
5/1970-1/1973	32	74
12/1987-7/1990	31	65
10/1966-11/1968	26	48
5/1947-6/1948	13	24

Graph recreated from information provided by: CFRA/S&P Global

But since the tech boom of the 90s, which saw the longest bull run in our market's history, things have changed.[69] A bull run is defined by prices that continue rising without being interrupted by the 20 percent decline that would signify a bear market.

With the 90s celebrating the advent of the internet and cell phones, global technology leading up to the year 2000, and the Y2K conversion of computer hardware and software, it was like a technological industrial revolution. The stock market reflected that fact from October 1990 through March 2000 when the S&P 500 grew by an unprecedented record of 417 percent.[70] But this new highest high was followed by three years of declines: 10.14 percent, 13.04 percent, and 23.37 percent in 2000, 2001, and 2002, respectively. Three straight years of declines had only previously occurred during the Great Depression and World War II.

The Great Recession – What Really Happened

Then, in late 2007, the markets, again, turned super volatile. Massive amounts of derivatives and mortgage-backed securities packaged as investment grade bonds lost a lot of value, causing liquidity to dry up and the housing market to crumble. Large financial institutions that wrote insurance policies protecting against the default of those bonds called credit default swaps, collapsed, or nearly collapsed. The U.S. GDP dropped by 0.3 percent in 2008 and another 2.8 percent in 2009. Unemployment hit 10 percent.[71]

It was the Great Recession... but it still hadn't reached the levels of the Great Depression in the 1930s. Not yet, anyway.

President George W. Bush signed the Troubled Asset Relief Program (TARP) in October 2008, which bought toxic assets from private financial institutions. Likewise, the Federal Reserve was determined to stave off a depression. The Fed initially used traditional means and reduced the federal funds rate from 5.25 percent in September 2007 to a range of 0 to .25 percent in December 2008.

However, with rates at or near zero, there was little interest rate changes left to leverage, so the Fed utilized nontraditional means and executed large scale asset purchases of mortgage backed securities from Fannie Mae and Freddie Mac and hundreds of billions in treasury securities by October 2009.[72]

This was quantitative easing, QE, of which there were three rounds in all—QE1, QE2, and QE3 — lasting for five years through October 2014. In the end, the Great Recession, lasting from December 2007 through June 2009, was the longest economic downturn since World War II.

Lower for Longer – Making History

Even though QE ended in 2014, the Fed continued to keep rates at their lowest levels ever for the longest amount of time ever which became known as "Lower for Longer." Slashing interest rates to help stimulate economic recovery was used outside the U.S. as well. Both the European Central Bank and the Bank of Japan used cheap monetary policy to stimulate economic recovery.[73]

Interest rates hit their lowest levels in 5,000 years of recorded history,[74] and in fact, in parts of the world like Japan[75] and Germany,[76] they were even negative!

Negative Interest Rates – The Rules Have Changed

Speaking of rules changing, for the first time in recorded history, we are seeing *negative* interest rates. Both Germany and Japan have issued 10-year bonds with a negative yield.[77]

But what does that mean?

With negative interest rates, you're paying the bank to store your money, just like you'd pay a monthly fee to store your furniture.

This is problematic because it puts a 5,000-year wedge in what we know to be true about finance. It calls everything into question. Banks have *always* paid you to hold your money because they can make money off of your money.

If that changes, everything we know about finance and compound interest changes. It's unfathomable.

The concept, albeit already demonstrated abroad, is so absurd that scholars from the world's more prestigious universities haven't even written papers about it yet!

Negative interest rates and their effect on your retirement are unprecedented and their effects are still unknown.

But why do we care about all of this? Why do we bother going through the Fed's economic actions, negative interest rates, and these bull and bear markets?

The answer is really quite simple.

This *New Normal* of major market volatility consists of really high highs followed by super low lows. The volatility of this *New Normal* since the 90s has changed, and will continue to change, the way America retires.

Record-breaking low interest rates mean investments aren't growing as quickly as they used to. Future retirees, specifically Baby Boomers, can no longer follow the traditional retirement model. They are no longer able to pull their money out of risk-based vehicles like the market to get a decent and safe return in the bank with a CD.

The result is a great and cruel irony.

The Great Irony

Retirees have felt trapped. Because of the Great Recession and the large portfolio losses that came with the market downturn, investors were forced to stay in the market if they had any hope of recovering their lost capital.

Retirees that wanted to leave the market that had lost them 57 percent from its October 2007 peak through its March 2009 trough, only had those record low-interest rates as a market alternative. Many were effectively stuck "chasing yield."

4 Percent Rule & The New Normal

Low-interest rates aren't the only reason retirement has changed in this *New Normal*. We financial advisors that have studied the effects of the "Lower for Longer" interest rates, combined with the *New Normal* of steep volatility, have also changed the way we calculate our client's ability to maintain their lifestyle during retirement.

In finance, the **4 percent rule** *was* the golden rule and refers to the annual retirement withdrawal percentage a retiree could expect to take from their portfolio and it last throughout retirement. At a 4 percent annual withdrawal rate of the retiree's total portfolio balance, a retiree used to be able to expect to receive a steady cash flow, year after year, for a 30 year period.[78]

The 4 percent rule was the metric most commonly accepted by the financial community until Morningstar published a report, "Low

Bond Yields and Safe Portfolio Withdrawal Rates," in 2013, establishing that the safe distribution rate had changed from the well-known 4 percent to a reduced 2.8 percent from the combination of low yields and market volatility.[79]

Suddenly, someone with a million-dollar retirement nest egg would only see $28,000 per year. And that's before taxes!

Most Americans are still building wealth based on the 4 percent rule, unaware that the rule has changed in this *New Normal. This standard change is HUGE and cannot be overstated.* If a retiree today wants to have the same probability of not outliving their retirement account as they used to, they would have to save 43 percent more under the lower 2.8 percent distribution rule.

Most financial advisors don't even know that the former 4 percent rule is no longer valid. If a retiree doesn't have an up-to-date advisor, and that retiree takes distributions based on the 4 percent rule, they have a 50/50 chance of running out of money.

It is critical that you ask yourself, "What kind of advisor do I have?"

Two Types of Advisors

Remember how we started this chapter with Mount Everest?

Getting to the summit is what we work our whole lives for, right? That summit is our moment of retirement. It's the moment when we put our money to work for us for the rest of our lives.

At that moment, we stop thinking about accumulation and start thinking about distribution. We start thinking about an exit strategy.

But how do you descend through your portfolio without consuming it all? How do you manage your retirement?

Here is where we see a clear divergence between financial advisors because there are really two different types in the world: the advisor that knows how to climb Everest and the advisor that knows how to get back down. In other words, some advisors specialize in growing wealth, while others are experts in distributing it. Some well-rounded advisors are capable of both expertise, but those are few and far between.

When I travel the country and talk with all kinds of people, one common question always comes up: "How do I know which type of advisor I have?"

It's actually quite simple. Does your advisor talk to you about Rate of Return, Return on Investment, Yield, and growing your portfolio to a certain number? Have they ever discussed how you will utilize your portfolio in retirement? Or do they just tell you that you can spend 4 percent per year and you will be fine?

Most advisors seem to be on the accumulation side of the equation.

I have had many clients that were initially quite reluctant to leave the advisor they had worked with for 30+ years. They're loyal and their advisor did a good job during the accumulation phase, helping them grow their portfolio.

But then I ask them, "Ok, but have you discussed a distribution plan? What's your exit strategy?"

In this age of a *New Normal*, your distribution strategy is just as important, if not more so, than what you did to accumulate your wealth in the first place. We are navigating a whole new world and an outdated rule just doesn't cut it anymore.

To have the most advantageous plan possible, some distribution strategies work best if you start to plan them five to 10 years before retirement.

The Luck of the Draw – A Special Risk

One of the most overlooked and volatility-specific risks is called **Sequence of Returns** risk. This is an especially nasty risk for those going into retirement because it can single-handedly cause your retirement plan to fail. You can literally do everything right in preparing for retirement and legitimately be ready to retire, and this one risk has the power to ruin everything!

The best way to illustrate this risk is to contrast two hypothetical couples, The Smiths and The Jones.

Each couple has a $500,000 market-based portfolio and are retiring at the age of 65. They both take 4 percent withdrawals annually, and increase that withdrawal by 3 percent annually to account for inflation. The Smiths experience the S&P 500 returns from 1979 through 2008 and the Jones experience the exact same returns only in reverse chronological order. Both couples want their portfolio to last through their planned 30 years of retirement.

Take a look at this chart.

Jones				Smith		
Hypothetical Net Return	Withdrawal	Balance	Age	Hypothetical Net Return	Withdrawal	Balance
		500,000	65			500,000
-35.61%	20,000	301,941	66	9.34%	20,000	526,676
2.16%	20,600	287,855	67	28.91%	20,600	658,362
11.65%	21,218	300,168	68	-9.98%	21,218	571,472
5.55%	21,855	294,974	69	12.71%	21,855	622,251
8.44%	22,510	297,372	70	18.58%	22,510	715,339
21.94%	23,185	339,432	71	0.81%	23,185	697,953
-21.27%	23,881	243,342	72	26.74%	23,881	860,705
-10.02%	24,597	194,358	73	17.59%	24,597	987,477
-11.82%	25,335	146,057	74	3.85%	25,335	1,000,166
18.49%	26,095	146,973	75	7.57%	26,095	1,049,765
25.95%	26,878	158,240	76	30.65%	26,878	1,344,630
32.30%	27,685	181,662	77	-9.24%	27,685	1,192,684
18.73%	28,515	187,177	78	27.82%	28,515	1,495,943
35.20%	29,371	223,698	79	4.34%	29,371	1,531,535
-1.36%	30,252	190,404	80	6.90%	30,252	1,607,026
6.90%	31,159	172,390	81	-1.36%	31,159	1,554,011
4.34%	32,094	147,782	82	35.20%	32,094	2,068,973
27.82%	33,057	155,835	83	18.73%	33,057	2,423,493
-9.24%	34,049	107,385	84	32.30%	34,049	3,172,152
30.65%	35,070	105,227	85	25.95%	35,070	3,960,376
7.57%	36,122	77,069	86	18.49%	36,122	4,656,671
3.85%	37,206	42,831	87	-11.82%	37,206	4,069,229
17.59%	38,322	12,041	88	-10.02%	38,322	3,623,118
26.74%	15,261	0	89	-21.27%	39,472	2,812,878
0.81%			90	21.94%	40,656	3,389,395
18.58%			91	8.44%	41,876	3,633,720
12.71%			92	5.55%	43,132	3,792,274
-9.98%			93	11.65%	44,426	4,189,602
28.91%			94	2.16%	45,759	4,234,225
9.34%			95	-35.61%	47,131	2,679,209
AVERAGE ANNUAL NET RETURN 9%						

While both couples have the exact same average 9 percent return over their 30-year retirement period, the Jones started retirement during an S&P 500 loss year, so that initial loss had a substantial impact on the ability of their portfolio to last throughout their retirement. So much so, in fact, that the Jones run completely out of money after 24 years and after receiving only $664,000 of total portfolio distributions, while the Smiths' retirement not only lasts for all 30 years, but their portfolio balance is over $2.6 million in the 30th year, even after taking $952,000 in total portfolio distributions.

This example illustrates perfectly that having accumulated the right amount in your portfolio for retirement, and even having a high average annual rate of return during retirement, cannot overcome the devastation to the success of your retirement plan that is caused by entering retirement right when your portfolio is decimated by a large S&P 500 downturn. With the *New Normal* of extremely high highs followed by extremely low lows, this one risk alone can destroy your retirement success.

Buy Low, Sell High

So, when is the appropriate time to cash out of the market? We have seen the utter lack of control we have over whether we enter retirement in a great up-year or a bad down-year and how that one fact alone can destroy our retirement dream. So, how do we gauge when to get out?

In the past, the answer was easy, but with record low interest rates and record setting highs, more and more investors are leery of pulling their money out of the market.

With these record-setting, all-time historic highs across the S&P 500, the Dow, and NASDAQ, I have really enjoyed asking every new potential client what their response was when their advisor called and asked if they wanted to actually realize their gains by selling? The response is the same every time, "Well, I never got that call. They have never asked me that."

Despite conventional wisdom, I haven't met anyone who has received that call from their broker. I have spoken with hundreds of people and not one has ever been asked about realizing and locking in their gain at these all-time highs.

Why is this the case when conventional wisdom is to buy low and sell high? Should we not sell at the highest highs the market has ever seen? If not at its highest, then when?

Greed and the Two Bone Syndrome

There is a childhood story of Aesop's Fable, *The Dog and His Reflection* about a dog that is a bit of a bully who one day takes a bone from his owner's table and runs off towards the river to eat it.

When he gets to the river, holding this big bone in his mouth, he sees another bone staring back at him. He really, really wants this other bone too, but he cannot get it because he is holding the first bone in his mouth.

So, what does he do? He drops the bone in his mouth into the river to get the second bone. And since the second bone was merely his reflection, he now has no bones at all.

This is precisely what the whole of America does with their portfolios before the market crashes. They do NOT want to sell now. Even with the highest highs the market has ever had – much like the bone in their mouth – they think they could make even more, so they don't want to sell.

They are suffering from something I like to call the "Two Bone Syndrome," based on the fable about greed. They take the risk of losing what they have in the hopes of still getting more!

And this, my friends, is exactly what America did during the Great Recession.

Buy and Hold and Missing Diamonds

We have been discussing when the appropriate time to sell would be given that conventional wisdom tells us to buy low and sell high. Naturally, the **Buy and Hold** philosophy comes up whenever one talks about liquidating their positions. Most advisors that preach 'Buy and Hold' through whatever conditions the market may bring, pair that advice by saying that over the long run, your money will come back as long as you hang in there long enough.

Let me be clear so as not to come across as being anti-market. This book is about how retirement has changed in America, and that is the perspective from which I am writing. When you are in your 20s, 30s, and 40s, and your investment horizon before retirement is sufficiently long enough, market downturns can actually work out favorably. You can buy in during the lows and ride your gains all the way to the top, so the Buy and Hold strategy works great in those age categories.

But when you are in the last 10 to 15 years before retirement, losing a significant amount of your portfolio to a market crash and taking years to retrieve what you already had is not a promising endeavor. After the loss from 2008 alone, it took the S&P 500 over four years to return to its pre-loss level.[80] If you only had 10 working years left with which to grow your money before retirement, you would have wasted more than 40 percent of that time just getting back to where you previously were.[81]

Does the picture of you running on a hamster wheel come to mind?

Like I mentioned in the previous chapter, losing my diamond was just like the Buy and Hold philosophy, and what advisors tell clients about waiting for your money to come back is simply often NOT true.

As we discussed in an earlier chapter, a portfolio loss of $100,000 turns into a loss of about $169,000 after nine years. Had that $100,000 been preserved and earning returns on average of 6 percent per year, that same loss equates to about $609,000 to your estate at your death.

So, even when your portfolio does eventually return to its former balance, it is not because the $100,000 loss was not a real loss, but because what you had left grew while you continued to contribute to your account.

Just because your portfolio returns to its former glory does not mean that you didn't experience a real financial loss, one that would have made your portfolio that much bigger had it been avoided in the first place.

The closer you get to retirement, the more dangerous the Buy and Hold strategy becomes simply because you have less time to make up for your losses. You have less time to earn your money back, and frankly, you need to make the most of that time by *growing* your money, rather than just recovering what you already had.

Volatility

Considering both volatility and the *New Normal*, is it appropriate to be 100 percent invested in the market?

Bull markets end when the bear awakens — and he always does. Since 1900, there have been 32 bear market corrections.[82] On average, a bear market comes approximately every 3.9 years, meaning your portfolio will lose 20 percent or more every 3.9 years.

So, if you lose 20 percent of your portfolio value every fourth year, what kind of odds are those for retirement? Nothing decimates the longevity of a portfolio faster than pulling money out of a financially depleted portfolio before it has had enough time to recover its losses. Pulling money out while it's down just compounds the effect of the sustained loss.

That's the terrifying power of volatility, and why it is a fundamental crack in the way most Americans retire today.

The market goes up, the market goes down. It's the nature of investing. It happens for all kinds of reasons, economic and otherwise, like geopolitical risks around the world.

Volatility is somewhat bearable if you're still far from retirement, but the closer you get to the summit, the less time you have to deal with losses. Additionally, having to pull money out during a down cycle and a down portfolio is the absolute worst thing you can do mathematically.

When you rely on the market, you leave your retirement up to chance. You are not in control.

In the old days, most Americans had pensions and Social Security to rely upon. Today, how much of your retirement is secure and guaranteed?

When it comes to planning for your retirement, you have two options: you can either play the market, leaving it all up to chance, or you can look at other vehicles that can give you solutions you can count on.

Can you count on the sequence of returns to be in your favor? Do you know what the sequence of returns will be when you retire? Are you comfortable knowing you may run out of funds 10 to 13 years after you retire should you be the unfortunate one to retire in a down cycle?

If you're not comfortable with that, then it's time to explore your options. You deserve peace of mind knowing your money is going to last as long as you need it.

We are living in uncertain times. It's time to take full control of your wealth and your retirement.

7 Fundamental Flaw #2 – Taxes

The Marshmallow Study

In the 1970s, the "Marshmallow Experiment," was conducted at Stanford University. The work focused on delayed gratification versus instant gratification.[83]

The study monitored more than 600 children from ages three to five. A child would be led into an empty, distraction-free room with a two-way mirror for observation. Each child was given a marshmallow.

"You can eat this marshmallow now," the adult would then say, "or you can wait, and when I come back, I'll bring you another one. Then you'll have two to eat."

As soon as the adult would leave the room, these children would start to squirm, wrestling with this decision: *do I wait and get more or do I eat what I have right in front of me?*

Some would turn away from the marshmallow so they couldn't see it, some would pull at their pigtails, and some would even kick the desk.

Others touched the marshmallow, or pretended to eat it, and some even took little nibbles.

Only a third of the children who attempted to delay gratification were successful while the rest ended up **caving** and eating their marshmallows before the adult returned.[84]

But this study didn't end that day. It actually followed these children and discovered several interesting correlations. The children that were able to delay gratification had higher overall SAT scores by a statistically significant amount,[85] lower BMIs (Body Mass Index),[86] and overall higher educational achievement,[87] leading to happier, more satisfied lives.[88]

In other words, the children that were able to wait became happier, more successful adults. Good things really do come to those who wait.

Hidden, Silent, Single Biggest Threat

I am sure you're wondering what the "Marshmallow Studies" have to do with taxes...

Everything!

As disruptive and damaging as volatility is, I actually believe that taxes — future taxes and future tax increases — will be *the* single biggest threat to your wealth and retirement security over the next 10 to 30 years. Taxes will be what destroys America's retirement dreams.

Why? Because with the widespread embrace nearly 40 years ago of accumulating wealth in pre-tax accounts, America forever tied building wealth with our unquenchable thirst for *instant gratification*. The pre-tax 401(k) has now ingrained new conditioning in America... in that the goal of saving and accumulating wealth alone is not in and of itself sufficient; now Americans want, need, and expect a tax reduction for doing it!

Instant Gratification

Here, instant gratification takes the form of a *tax deferral* — which ironically will be the very thing that will end up destroying most of America's retirement dreams.

Like I mentioned earlier in the book, the 401(k) was initially created as a way for corporate executives and highly compensated employees to dodge taxes, on top of their generous pensions. Pre-tax contributions lowered their overall annual income, thereby reducing their tax burden for that year. The 401(k)'s rollout to all employees as their main retirement savings, in lieu of their pension, happened by accident.[89]

In the 80s, many companies and employees of all compensation levels began investing in and relying on the 401(k) as their main retirement vehicle. Where a pension had no impact on a worker's monthly paycheck, utilizing a 401(k) would lower their taxes and suddenly people were deferring taxes left and right, preferring the instant gratification of an immediately lower tax bill.[90]

And now, most of America is planning on retiring with money from these pre-tax accounts.

But like everything that happens by accident, thought and planning did not go into this massive American financial shift (phenomenon, really) that changed the way America retires. And a whole new way of thinking about retirement and taxes began to justify planning for retirement with pre-tax dollars – thoughts which have since become the conventional wisdom America has believed for the last 35+ years.

Idiotic Loan

Imagine for a moment that you need money.

So, you call your friend or your family member and you say that you just need to borrow a few thousand dollars. Your friend/family member comes straight over with a check, but they have written in the memo line "LOAN."

Now, before you accept this 'loan' you want to know a few things. You ask your helper, "Well, how much do you want me to repay and by when?" Only seems logical that you would want to know the terms of this loan.

But what if your friend or family member said, "You know what – right now I am doing really good, and I do not need this money. But I tell you what. Some day in the future, when I do need money, I am going to come back to you, see how much money you have then, and then I will tell you how much you have to pay me back."

Now, how many of you would accept a loan with such open-ended and ridiculous terms, never having any idea how much of your future wealth it would cost you? No rational person would accept this loan.

Who Really Wins Here?

Everyone agrees that accepting a loan in which the terms will not be defined until some point in the future (which is then based on your future wealth) is not a loan they would take. But this is *exactly* what every single person utilizing a pre-tax retirement account is doing.

Let's say that you made $100,000 this year in income. Assume the tax rate is a flat 20 percent, ignoring exemptions and deductions. By that math, you rightly owe the government $20,000.

But the government is offering you a deal! If you take $20,000 dollars and put it in a pre-tax retirement vehicle like a 401(k) — although you can actually only contribute $18,000 per year as of 2017 — excluding the catch-up provisions, you will only pay taxes on a salary of $80,000.

That means you will pay $16,000 in taxes, a difference of $4,000.

Now, most people (even CPAs) think of this $4,000 as a 'tax-savings,' a few will call it a tax deferral, but the United States Treasury Department considers it a loan.

If I owed the U.S. Treasury $20,000 on my current $100,000 earnings and I only pay $16,000, that is $4,000 of extra money that I have in my bank account not paid to the IRS that has been loaned to me by the government. This would be instant gratification, like eating the first marshmallow immediately.

However, that $4,000 has to be paid back at some point in the future. And what, may I ask, are the terms of this government loan? What rate will you be paying and how much do you have to pay them back?

You do not know! You won't know for years until you actually retire and have to pay the money back. Only then will you know the tax rate at which you must repay this loan.

Also, when you repay the government, the repayment amount will not just be based on the original $4,000 loan, but on the full amount you have saved in that pre-tax account.

The terms of this loan are mysteriously absent. You have no idea how much you will actually owe; you simply know you will owe *at least* $4,000, unless your portfolio actually loses value, which is not a desirable tax strategy.

Let's see what could happen and expand on this example.

Over the next 20 years, your original, pre-tax investment triples from $20,000 to $60,000.

Let's say that the tax rate only increases by a modest 10 percent (we will tackle this later).

At a 30 percent tax rate, when you withdraw your $60,000, you pay a tax of $18,000.

So, you tripled your money from $20,000 to $60,000, but the government more than quadrupled their share from $4,000 to $18,000.

Who really wins here?

You might be thinking that you won't take all $60,000 out at one time, so you won't have to pay such a large tax.

But is that true?

If you are using this pre-tax account to replace your income, in addition to Social Security, will you not be withdrawing a substantial amount per year? The National Academy of Social Insurance states that medium-level income earners will have approximately 40 percent of their wages replaced by Social Security payments and high-level earners will have about 26 percent replaced by Social Security payments.[91] That leaves you to replace anywhere from 60 percent to 74 percent of your pre-retirement salary yourself. That seems like a pretty sizable annual withdrawal and resulting tax to me.

We admittedly do not know what future tax rates will be, so let's review what we do know.

What We Do Know Now and What That Means for Later

First, we know that the ordinary income tax is the *highest* tax we have under the U.S. Tax Code, and we know that this is the tax that will apply in retirement to all our pre-tax accounts. This special kind of pre-tax money will be subjected to whatever the ordinary income tax rate is *at the time that money is withdrawn.*

Second, we know that the United States is in the worst fiscal position ever in its history, caused primarily by two occurrences we'll discuss later in this chapter.

Third, we know that we only win the pre-tax "game" if tax rates either stay the same and we make less money or tax rates go down. So, in order to pay less tax in retirement, we are essentially betting that our income will be lower or that taxes will decrease.

But how else could we lose this bet?

Government Overspending & Retirement Plans

What impact does the overspending of our federal government have on the success or failure of our retirement plan? Well, as our national debt continues to grow, it is more than just likely that our tax rates will go up. Much like the *Titanic* analogy I used earlier, at some point it becomes a *mathematical certainty.*

And because the government has inextricably tied tax policy to America's overall retirement strategy, as the government goes, so goes the state of America's retirement. We have been conditioned for 35-plus years to believe that we should be getting tax benefits *now*, while we are working and not later during our golden retirement years. This has led America to now expect a tax incentive in order to properly accumulate retirement wealth. And this has ensured that the government is your silent partner inside of your retirement account.

There are some recent examples of just how wrong this can go…

Poland – Getting It Wrong

In September 2013, Poland confiscated and nationalized half of the assets held in private pension plans in order to cut their own sovereign debt.[92] Then in July 2016, the country announced its plan to disassemble its privately-owned pension system.[93]

As we discussed earlier in this book, relying on the government for anything is problematic. Entrepreneurship and free market systems promote competition and economic growth, but it looks as though Poland is advocating the exact opposite.[94]

The country is distributing hand-outs by way of a government-funded pension plan, but of course the real source of funding is the already funded private pension system, as the government is not the creator of anything but merely a distributor of what exists privately.

Government is always a taker: a taker from one to transfer it to another for whatever purpose they feel worthy. Government is necessary and has a vital purpose, but they are not a net real economic creator.

In this instance, the Polish government is essentially promising to pay their people the equivalent of what they would have otherwise had in the private market. What if the Polish government doesn't generate enough tax revenue to keep their pension promises? The Polish government effectively nationalized private wealth. The concept should scare us all.

Challenging Conventional Wisdom

Do you know that some people — perhaps many Americans even — somehow think they won't have to pay any taxes in retirement, that they have somehow deferred taxes permanently?

This is a major misconception!

You don't get to avoid paying taxes on pre-tax accumulations — ever. Nothing magical happens when you retire and start collecting Social Security. Deferring your taxes truly means that you are promising to pay them later, no matter your age or station in life. The tax man always cometh!

So why defer at all?

Conventional wisdom, which came about in the late 70s and early 80s with the wide acceptance and implementation of the 401(k) as a replacement to the company pension, tells us that we will likely make less money when we retire.

The funny thing is, most of my clients want to maintain their current lifestyles in retirement. Meaning they want and plan on having roughly the same cash flow in retirement as they do before retirement.

In fact, I have never once had a client come to me and say, "Rebecca, I want to have about 30 percent less income in retirement than I have right now, and we are excited about living on just 70 percent of what we have been used to living on for these last 20 years."

The reality is that people do not want to downgrade their lifestyles.

When we look at this conventional wisdom about making less and therefore paying less, we see that it came about during a very different America than the America of 2017. Our National Debt was just reaching the $1 trillion threshold for the first time in 1981,[95] due to Nixon ditching the gold standard in August of 1971. Thus, unfettered printing of debt had not previously been possible.[96]

At the same time, the Baby Boomers were between 16 years and 34 years old, so no one was thinking about the impact of their eventual retirement, en masse, as a whole generation in 1980. Had we actually planned a strategic, mathematically sound alternative to the former company pension system, the Baby Boomer retirement dilemma would most certainly have been a consideration.

But alas, sometimes things that come about accidentally also come with

Historical Debt Outstanding - Annual 1970 - 2015

DATE	DOLLAR AMOUNT
09/30/2015	18,150,617,666,484.33
09/30/2014	17,824,071,380,733.82
09/30/2013	16,738,183,526,697.32
09/30/2012	16,066,241,407,385.89
09/30/2011	14,790,340,328,557.15
09/30/2010	13,561,623,030,891.79
09/30/2009	11,909,829,003,511.75
09/30/2008	10,024,724,896,912.49
09/30/2007	9,007,653,372,262.48
09/30/2006	8,506,973,899,215.23
09/30/2005	7,932,709,661,723.50
09/30/2004	7,379,052,696,330.32
09/30/2003	6,783,231,062,743.62
09/30/2002	6,228,235,965,597.16
09/30/2001	5,807,463,412,200.06
09/30/2000	5,674,178,209,886.86
09/30/1999	5,656,270,901,615.43
09/30/1998	5,526,193,008,897.62
09/30/1997	5,413,146,011,397.34
09/30/1996	5,224,810,939,135.73
09/29/1995	4,973,982,900,709.39
09/30/1994	4,692,749,910,013.32
09/30/1993	4,411,488,883,139.38
09/30/1992	4,064,620,655,521.66
09/30/1991	3,665,303,351,697.03
09/28/1990	3,233,313,451,777.25
09/29/1989	2,857,430,960,187.32
09/30/1988	2,602,337,712,041.16
09/30/1987	2,350,276,890,953.00
09/30/1986	2,125,302,616,658.42
09/30/1985	1,823,103,000,000.00
09/30/1984	1,572,266,000,000.00
09/30/1983	1,377,210,000,000.00
09/30/1982	1,142,034,000,000.00
09/30/1981	997,855,000,000.00
09/30/1980	907,701,000,000.00
09/30/1979	826,519,000,000.00
09/30/1978	771,544,000,000.00
09/30/1977	698,840,000,000.00
06/30/1976	620,433,000,000.00
06/30/1975	533,189,000,000.00
06/30/1974	475,059,815,731.55
06/30/1973	458,141,605,312.09
06/30/1972	427,260,460,940.50
06/30/1971	398,129,744,455.54
06/30/1970	370,918,706,949.93

https://www.treasurydirect.gov/govt/reports/pd/histdebt/histdebt.htm

unanticipated and unconsidered consequences — even if those consequences take years to rear their ugly head.

The Perfect Storm

Fast forward from the 80s to present day. Picture two massive storms crashing and colliding together to make one monstrous "Perfect Storm."

Let's look at what these storms are…

A Genius System – Storm #1

When I think of Social Security, the last thing that comes to mind is how ingeniously it was designed. But initially it was.

When President Franklin D. Roosevelt first enacted it in 1935, the retirement age for benefits was 65 years old, but the average mortality age for women and men was 65.2 and 62 years, respectively. In fact, only 53.9 percent of all males who reached age 21 even survived until age 65, and only 60.6 percent of all females who reached age 21 survived until age 65.

Year Cohort Turned 65	Percentage of Population Surviving from Age 21 to Age 65		Average Remaining Life Expectancy for Those Surviving to Age 65	
	Male	Female	Male	Female
1940	53.9	60.6	12.7	14.6
1950	56.2	65.5	13.1	16.2
1960	60.1	71.3	13.2	17.4
1970	63.7	76.9	13.8	18.6
1980	67.8	80.9	14.6	19.1
1990	72.3	83.6	15.3	19.6

Therefore, even for those that paid into the system, less than 60 percent of the population would live long enough to receive their benefits.[97]

Even those people who *did* receive the benefit did not receive it much beyond 10 years before they, too, passed away.

Mathematically, the system was very sound.

Today, the same system is far different.

First of all, the retirement age has roughly remained the same, having increased by only two years to age 67, even though life expectancy has increased by roughly 20 years. So now, almost everyone winds up getting Social Security for about 20 years instead of a fraction of people receiving it for only 10! This rate of Social Security benefit payments is mathematically unsustainable.

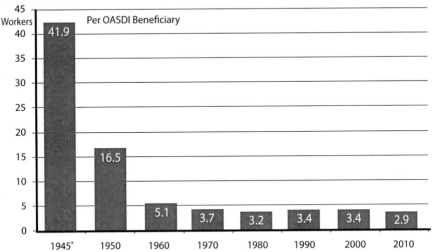

Graph recreated from information provided by: 2012 OASDI Trustee report, Social Security Administration.
Data note: The Trustee Report provides data from 1945 and onward. Prior estimates are unavailable.

In 1945, we had about 42 people paying into the system for every one person on benefits. In 2010, that same ratio was three to one. By the time the last Baby Boomer retires in 2030, it is expected to be even more severe. Projections suggest that there will be fewer than two people paying in for every one person on benefits.[98]

We have about 10,000 Baby Boomers retiring every single day from today through the year 2030.[99] When a boomer retires from working, they are considered a "double negative" to the federal budget. The first negative comes just from their retirement because they were previously paying into and contributing to the federal budget through both income taxes and payroll taxes. The second negative impact to the federal budget comes when they go onto Medicare and start receiving Social Security income.

The financial impact of the en masse retirement of our largest organic-born generation cannot be overstated.

Social Security is the sacred cow of American politics but the federal government cannot conquer math nor pretend its rules do not apply to them, as much as they would like to.

In my practice, unless a client is a Baby Boomer, we do not even include Social Security income in their retirement projections. We realize that, at the very least, benefits will have to be tested according to their means. In fact, this has already begun with the up to 85 percent taxation of Social Security payments to beneficiaries, based upon the amount of the beneficiary's other income. The official Trustee's report for Social Security and Medicare in 2017 reveals that the unfunded liability for Social Security is about $15 trillion and the unfunded liability for Medicare is about $100 trillion — a figure that is literally too hard to comprehend. The writing is on the wall for those who choose to read it.

David Walker – Storm #2

Most people have never heard the name David Walker. Mr. Walker served as the U.S. Comptroller General from 1998 to 2008. He was appointed by President Bill Clinton and served under both Clinton and George W. Bush.[100]

During the last year of his tenure, the Congressional Budget Office (CBO) authored a reported entitled "The Long-Term Economic Effects of Some Alternative Budget Policies,"[101] in which they discussed the spending on the three main social programs of Social Security, Medicare, and Medicaid.

In the report, the CBO states unequivocally that to maintain projected spending, "the tax rate for the lowest tax bracket would have to be increased from 10 percent to 25 percent; that tax rate on incomes in the current 25 percent bracket would have to be increased to 63 percent; and the tax rate of the highest bracket would have to be raised from 35 percent to 88 percent."

The cover letter of the report alone, written to then Representative Paul Ryan, was equally disturbing. CBO Director Peter Orszag writes, "Rising costs for health care and the aging of the population will cause federal spending on Medicare, Medicaid, and Social Security to rise substantially as a share of the economy. If tax revenues as a share of gross domestic product (GDP) remain at current levels, that additional spending will eventually cause future budget deficits to become unsustainable."

"TO PREVENT THOSE DEFICITS FROM GROWING TO LEVELS THAT COULD IMPOSE SUBSTANTIAL COSTS ON THE ECONOMY, THE CHOICES ARE LIMITED: *REVENUES MUST RISE AS A SHARE OF GDP, PROJECTED SPENDING MUST FALL, OR BOTH.*" In other words, taxes MUST go up and benefit payments MUST go down. I added the emphasis to this section myself because it is so incredibly important to understand.

Please read the letter for yourself below and when you do, remember that this was written in 2008 and our national debt was only $10.6 trillion on President Bush's last day in office in January 2009.

As of this writing, and separate and apart from our underfunded social programs, we have national debt in excess of $20 trillion dollars. The U.S. Government must get the funds to service that debt from somewhere.

CONGRESSIONAL BUDGET OFFICE
U.S. Congress
Washington, DC 20515

Peter R. Orszag, Director

May 19, 2008

Honorable Paul Ryan
Ranking Member
Committee on the Budget
U.S. House of Representatives
Washington, DC 20515

Dear Congressman:

Under current law, rising costs for health care and the aging of the population will cause federal spending on Medicare, Medicaid, and Social Security to rise substantially as a share of the economy. If tax revenues as a share of gross domestic product (GDP) remain at current levels, that additional spending will eventually cause future budget deficits to become unsustainable. To prevent those deficits from growing to levels that could impose substantial costs on the economy, the choices are limited: Revenues must rise as a share of GDP, projected spending must fall, or both.

In response to your letter of May 15, 2008, the Congressional Budget Office (CBO) has prepared the attached analysis of the potential economic effects of (1) allowing federal debt to climb as projected under the alternative fiscal scenario presented in CBO's *The Long-Term Budget Outlook* (December 2007), (2) slowing the growth of deficits and then eliminating them over the next several decades, and (3) using higher income tax rates alone to finance the increases in spending projected under the alternative fiscal scenario. In keeping with CBO's mandate to provide objective, impartial analysis, this report makes no policy recommendations.

CBO would be pleased to address any further questions you have. I can be reached at (202) 226-2700. The staff contact for the macroeconomic analysis is Doug Hamilton, who can be reached at (202) 226-2770; the contact for the tax analysis is David Weiner, who can be reached at (202) 226-2689.

Sincerely,

Peter R. Orszag

Attachment

cc: Honorable John M. Spratt Jr.
      Chairman

Those predictions were based on numbers and simulations from 2008. Our debt is considerably higher today.

The bottom line is, from a mathematical perspective, taxes *will* increase. Politics and politicians can operate in the gray area all they would like, but math is black and white. It's infallible. It's absolute and always correct. That is what I love about it.

The math tells me, David Walker, and the CBO that taxes *must* go up. It's just that simple.

Conventional Wisdom Has It Wrong

Some might believe that they will pay less in taxes in retirement by earning less income, but that logic is based solely on what one is earning and provides no consideration for any change to tax rates. In fact, it assumes that tax rates either stay the same or even go down.

One question I always ask clients is whether they feel like they would be better able to handle tax increases during their working years or during their retirement years, when they are not working and more likely to be on a fixed income.

Additionally, during the working years, most of us are likely to still have children at home that count as tax exemptions, and have a mortgage whose related interest can be an itemized deduction. There are dozens of ways to help reduce taxes in our active working years but, once we retire, the children and their exemptions are gone, and hopefully, the mortgage has been paid off.

Since we are not working during retirement, rising taxes could force us to take on part-time work if we want to maintain our pre-retirement lifestyle. There seems to be a definite drop in options once we are retired and on a more fixed income.

So, we see that deferring taxes only becomes a benefit if tax rates stay the same or go down. When tax rates rise, you could make less and still pay more in taxes.

And really, besides the instant gratification of paying less in taxes this year, why wouldn't we just go ahead and pay the taxes now? Why would we ever bet on future tax rates given the America of 2017?

Taxes on Sale

Many Americans truly believe that tax rates cannot really go up. They have been lulled by the low tax rates we have enjoyed since 1987, where the top rate has always been less than 50 percent.[102]

But, if you actually look at our tax history, you will see that these last 30 years are actually an anomaly in that history. Since World War II, we've been in our third-lowest tax bracket period ever.

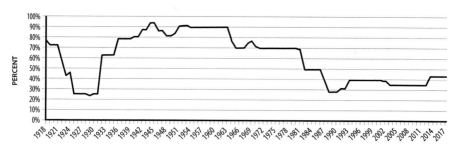

History of Tax Rates: 1913-2017

Top Federal Tax Rates

Graph recreated from information provided by: Bradford Tax Institute

Over the last 100 years, the highest tax rate has averaged 61 percent. Today, our top tax rate is 39.6 percent, meaning that current taxes are actually discounted by more than 20 percent, relative to the last 100 years.[103]

So, why would anyone want to defer paying taxes during this super-low tax rate period? Why would anyone gamble on taxes being lower in the future verses their current atypical lows, given the perfect storm of the Baby Boomer retirement wave and the increasing national debt that is brewing?

You're going to have to pay the taxes eventually. That has been established. Considering taxes are at an almost all-time low and America is fast approaching the worst fiscal position in which it has ever been, gambling on future tax rates becomes nonsensical.

TOP FEDERAL INCOME TAX RATES SINCE 1913
(top brackets in nominal dollars)

YEAR	TOP REGULAR RATES WAGES & OTHER EARNED	UNEARNED EXCEPT CAP GAINS	ABOVE TAXABLE INC. (JOINT) OF	CAPITAL GAINS MAX.	CAPITAL GAINS TAXATION
1913-15	7%	7%	$ 500,000	15%	Realized gains taxed same as other income
1916	15%	15%	2,000,000	15%	"
1917	67%	67%	2,000,000	67%	"
1918	77%	77%	1,000,000	77%	"
1919-21	73%	73%	1,000,000	73%	"
1922	58%	58%	200,000	12.5%	Maximum rate
1923	43.5%	43.5%	200,000	12.5%	"
1924	46%	46%	500,000	12.5%	"
1925-28	25%	25%	100,000	12.5%	"
1929	24%	24%	100,000	12.5%	"
1930-31	25%	25%	100,000	12.5%	"
1932-33	63%	63%	1,000,000	12.5%	"
1934-35	63%	63%	1,000,000	31.5%	Sliding exclusion of 70%>10 yrs; 0%<1 yr.
1936-37	78%	78%	2,000,000	39%	"
1938-40	78%	78%	2,000,000	30%	Excl. 50%>2yrs; 67% 18-24mo; 0%<18mo; 30%Max
1941	80%	80%	2,000,000	30%	"
1942-43	88%	88%	200,000	25%	Exclusion 50% > 6 months; 25% maximum
1944-45	94%	94%	200,000	25%	"
1946-47	86.5%	86.5%	200,000	25%	"
1948-49	82.1%	82.1%	200,000	25%	"
1950	84.4%	84.4%	200,000	25%	"
51-64	91%	91%	200,000	25%	"
64-67	70%	70%	200,000	25%	"
1968	75.3%	75.3%	200,000	26.9%	Transition
1969	77%	77%	200,000	27.5%	"
1970	50%	70%	200,000	32.3%	"
1971	50%	70%	200,000	34.3%	"
1972-75	50%	70%	200,000	36.5%	50% exclusion, minimum tax effects
1976-77	50%	70%	203,200	39.9%	"
1978	50%	70%	203,200	39%	"
1979-80	50%	70%	215,400	28%	60% exclusion
1981	50%	70%	215,400	23.7%	50% or 60% exclusion, etc.,transition
1982	50%	50%	85,600	20%	60% exclusion
1983	50%	50%	109,400	20%	"
1984-86	50%	50%	168,900	20%	"
1987	38.5%	38.5%	90,000	28%	Maximum rate
1988-90*	28%/33%	28%/33%	*	28%/33%	Realized gains taxed same as other income
1991-92	31.9%	31.9%	84,100	28.9%	Maximum rate
1993-96	43.7%	40.8%	255,100	29.2%	"
1997-2000	43.7%	40.8%	275,000	21.2%	"
2001	43.2%	40.3%	297,350	21.2%	"
2002	42.7%	39.8%	307,050	21.2%	18% top capital gains rate in rare cases
2003-05	39.0%	36.1%	319,200	16.1%	Reduced maximum rate, which also applied to dividends
2006-07	38.6%	35.7%	343,100	15.7%	"
2008-09	38.3%	35.4%	365,300	15.4%	"
2010-12	37.9%	35.0%	379,300	15%	"
2013-on	44.6%	44.6%	390,100	25%	21.2% income tax plus 3.8% Medicare tax; also on dividends
*1988-90 detail:	28% 33% 28%	28% 33% 28%	31,050 75,050 155,780	28% 33% 28%	

Notes:
1. 1991-2009 and post 2010 rates include the tax-rate effects of the personal exemption phase-out and the partial itemized deduction disallowan enacted in 1990. These provisions began to be phased out in 2006, were eliminated in 2010-12, and are scheduled to be reinstated in 2013.
2. 1993-2012 top regular rates on earned income include the 2.9% Medicare tax.
3. 2013-on top rates include the 3.8% Medicare tax on most earned *and* unearned income for high-income taxpayers enacted in 2010, and the scheduled expiration of the Bush tax cuts after 2012.
4. The definition of taxable income varied very substantially over the years. Taxable income is always substantially below actual income.
5. For multi-year periods with indexed tax brackets (post-1984) the top-bracket starting points are the averages for the periods.
Graph recreated from information provided by: Citizens for Tax Justice, November 2011.

Always Two Yous

For every dollar you earn, there are actually two people to consider: your current self and your future self. The more your current self spends of that dollar, the less your future self will have to spend, right?

When you choose to save on taxes now by deferring their payment to later, you aren't thinking about your future self.

For those Americans that are dead-set on using pre-tax retirement accounts, their current self is winning over their future self because they're addicted to current tax savings. It's like a drug to them.

Auto-Enrollment, Auto-Escalation, & Even State Run Plans...

Unfortunately, instead of retreating from the failures of the 401(k), the government and private employers seem to be doubling down, encouraging, and even pushing more people to sign up through the auto-enrollment of new employees, auto-escalation of pre-tax contributions of participating employees, and even state-run plans for those that have no pre-tax option with their private employer.[104] This will only continue to increase the usage and reliance on the 401(k) and its related cousins, the 403(b) and the 457, as America's retirement vehicle of choice, making this book all the more relevant and important.

Think back to the last time you had to complete new hire paperwork. Do you remember how easy it was to enroll in the company's 401(k) plan? All you had to do was fill in a few lines of info, check a couple of boxes, and sign on the line, right?

Many clients ask, "But what about the match my employer makes?"

Obviously, we do not want to walk away from "free" money so my general answer is to contribute to the match and then maximize your alternative retirement strategy.

However, even that general answer has to be qualified with some tax analysis projecting how much ordinary income you already expect to have during retirement. This should include any pension, rental income, dividends, interest and capital gains, and social security.

If those sources of income are putting you well into the taxable income brackets, then adding an additional source of ordinary income may push you into the next highest income bracket, causing the tax you pay on your other income to effectively increase. This analysis is revealed in tax projections we prepare for our clients.

Roth as an Alternative

In addition to 401(k)s, some companies now offer Roth 401(k)s.

Roth 401(k)s allow for post-tax contributions, meaning you pay your taxes now as opposed to later. But unlike just using an after-tax brokerage account, both the principal and all its growth remains tax-free as long as you play by the government's rules.

Those rules include a five-year seasoning requirement of the account, and you must be age 59 1/2 before you can access your gains tax free. You can always withdraw your contributions penalty and tax free, but you cannot access the growth without paying tax and a penalty if you have not had the Roth for five years and you are not 59 1/2 years of age.[105]

These plans, from a tax perspective, are a superior choice to the traditional 401(k). However, because of the volatility of the market, which we covered in depth in the last chapter, they should be used in conjunction with another retirement strategy as well.

Many companies do not offer Roth 401(k)s because the company's matching contribution would still be placed in a traditional 401(k), causing additional administrative burdens. So, do not be surprised when you cannot get both your contribution and the company's into a Roth.

The Newest Trend - 409As

Before we move on, I want to make sure we discuss a new trend: 409A plans.

One of my clients, Claire, is a doctor. We had a meeting last week and she told me that the hospital she works for has her on a 409A (known as a 409A Nonqualified Deferred Compensation Plan [NQDC]).

Never heard of a 409A? The IRS defines it as such:

> "Section 409A applies to compensation that workers earn in one year, but that is paid in a future year. This is referred to as nonqualified deferred compensation."[106]

Simply put, these plans allow for highly compensated employees to defer taxes on up to 50 percent of their salaries.

Claire makes about $200,000 a year. A 409A allows her to defer taxes on up to $100,000 of her salary. She doesn't get a match, like with a 401(k), but her annual, taxable income is cut in half.

Sounds great for today, but what happens to her money tomorrow?

These plans, deferred compensation plans for highly compensated employees, are coming out in droves, because many highly-compensated Americans are attracted to the idea of saving half their income now, tax-free… or so they think.

But deferring taxes on half of your income for 20 to 30 years is actually a terrible tax strategy!

When tax rates increase — as we have established that they must - you will end up paying more taxes on more money because the account will have also grown by being invested. Therefore, 409As are even worse than 401(k)s.

What a nightmare!

Greatest Transfer of Wealth in the History of the World

We are on the precipice of the largest transfer of wealth in the history of the world. In the next 15 years, $30 trillion will be moving down from one generation to the next.[107] And what makes this transfer even more impactful is that a large portion of that money is currently housed in pre-tax qualified accounts.[108]

Total Retirement assets were $25 trillion in 2015 — with the greatest share in pre-tax IRAs of $7.6 trillion, and with another $6.8 trillion in defined contribution plans like the 401(k), which alone had $4.7 trillion.

So, pre-tax accounts are $14.4 trillion of the $24.9 trillion in retirement assets. An additional $8.3 trillion is in pension plans, with $3.2 trillion in private plans and $5.1 trillion in government pensions. This is an additional $8.3 trillion in pre-tax accounts since pensions are taxed as ordinary income for the recipient's entire life.

These 3 categories — IRAs, 401(k)s, and pensions — are all pre-tax and equal $22.7 trillion of the $25 trillion total making American retirement accounts 91 percent pre-tax accounts![109]

This means that nearly all of that money has yet to be taxed.

Do you think the U.S. government is counting on that? You bet they are.

In fact, they must.

The U.S. Debt Clock shows that our national debt exceeds $20 trillion. But towards the middle of the screen, you can see that the total U.S. debt is listed as more than $67 trillion. That's a debt of almost $210,000 *per person.*[110]

It's incomprehensible... and yet, true.

Again, taxes simply *must* go up and those funds in pre-tax accounts will take a big hit.

Required Minimum Distribution (RMDs)

We already know pre-tax accounts are taxed at the highest tax possible in America, the ordinary income tax, right? We also know that it is highly likely that taxes will go up over the next 10 years or so because of the retirement of the Boomers and our unbelievable national debt.

But let's say you're retired now, or plan on retiring within the next few years. Hypothetically, you have all your wealth in pre-tax accounts. You've kept it all in the market, had a great run of luck, and have doubled your money. You now have $2 million worth of assets off of which you are living. Not only have you worked hard to grow this account, you've also been meticulous with your calculations. There's no way you're running out of money.

So, what happens when you die? How is your wealth distributed?

Do you believe your heirs will simply roll the money over into another pre-tax account, called a stretch-IRA? Do you believe your heirs will continue to let the account grow until he or she needs the funds for their own retirement?

Let's say that is precisely what happens (statistically, that isn't likely but we'll get into that in a moment). Your heirs let the account grow and grow and grow. 20 years later, it's valued at a whopping $4 million. On paper, it sure looks like you did everything right.

The problem is that when your heirs turn 70 1/2 years old, he or she will be forced to withdraw a **required minimum distribution** (RMD) on that $4 million. If the tax rate really reaches 88 percent, that $4 million quickly becomes only $480,000.

All that growth, including the growth you experienced while you were alive, would be completely demolished. At an 88 percent tax rate, your heirs would be left with less than even what *you* started with.

You may be getting a break now, but your heirs, your children and your childrens' children, will end up paying a lot more later on. That is no way to build solid intergenerational wealth. In fact, utilizing the government as your family's wealth building partner via pre-tax accounts is like asking the fox to guard the hen house.

Found Money Syndrome

Remember when I said that, statistically, it would be unlikely for an heir to roll-over a pre-tax account into a stretch-IRA? According to the IRS, roughly 90 percent of all inherited pre-tax accounts will be cashed out within six months of death.[111] People don't roll these accounts over, but choose, instead, to cash them out thanks to the "Found Money Syndrome."

One of my clients, Marie, has over $2 million in an IRA. She has accumulated wealth through various positions throughout her career and has let the account grow.

Marie is very scrupulous and isn't a big spender. When it came time to discuss tax planning, she insisted it wasn't necessary. She could live off her money for the rest of her life. That was all she needed to know.

"You know, Marie, you're not really spending this money. This is $2 million dollars. If you continue to grow it, by the time you die, it could reach $3 million. Then what happens?" I asked her one day.

"My only son, John, will inherit it," she told me.

"What do you think he'll do with it?" I asked.

"He'll cash it out."

"If he cashes it out, how much do you think he'll get?"

She pinched her eyebrows together and grabbed her chin, thinking. After a few moments, she said, "Over $2.5 million."

"Out of $3 million, you think John will get more than $2.5 million? What if I told you he would get less than that? What if I told you he would get about $1.8 million?"

Her jaw dropped. She was shocked. "What?"

"Yes, if he cashes it out in one lump sum, he's going to pay a 40 percent tax."

Marie sat there silently for a moment. I could tell that it really bothered her that the government would get that much of her hard-earned cash.

The problem is that her son, John, likely won't care that he'll lose $1.2 million because he'll be gaining $1.8 million. This is the "found money syndrome," in which you don't care about how much is going to the government, because it is all new money to you. And that's what the government is counting on.

Take Back Control

Taxes have the power to destroy your wealth accumulation and retirement dreams, but if you take control, you can mitigate those losses.

You have a lot more control over your wealth while you're young and working. From a pure tax strategies standpoint, when you're young and working, you can manipulate and control your annual income tax. If you own a home and pay a mortgage, you can take a mortgage interest deduction. If you have children or dependents you can take a deduction for them, also.

In contrast, when you're retired, you're on a fixed income. It's likely that your house will be paid off, meaning you'll no longer have that mortgage interest deduction. And unless you have an in-law living with you, it is unlikely that you will have any dependents.

So, you will have a decrease in exemptions, a decrease in deductions, and a decreased ability to manipulate and control your income tax.

If you're 35 and your tax rate goes up, you can get a second job flipping burgers if you must. But when you're on a fixed income and the tax rate goes up, your options are limited.

Would you rather control taxes when you're working and earning money or when you're on a fixed income?

The Caterpillar and the Tax Burn

I heard a story once of two brothers who were outside playing on a hot summer day when they came across a cocoon hanging from a tree branch. The cocoon was moving so they stopped for a minute to watch.

They saw a crack form in the cocoon and stared as it shook and moved. They finally realized that the bug inside was trying to escape, but seemed to be having a rather difficult time of it.

After a long time, the brothers decided to help the bug out. They took the cocoon from the tree and brought it to their front porch. They took a very small stick and began to help the bug make its escape route larger. Just then their Dad returned home from work.

"What are you boys doing?" he asked.

The boys explained that the bug was trying to escape but that it was stuck inside, so they had brought him over to the porch to get him out.

"Oh no!" their Dad responded. "No, no boys! That is a caterpillar inside which has turned into a butterfly with brand new wings. Because its wings are new and have never been used before, it must work very hard to wiggle its way out of the cocoon. It is in the wiggling, in the struggle, that its wings will grow strong enough so that once it does break through, it will be able to fly. Without the struggle, its wings will not be strong enough to support its weight, and I am afraid now it will never fly."

It is in the struggle that we become strong enough to handle what comes our way. It is in the struggle that we will often find and fulfill our destiny. It is in the struggle that we become our most refined, strongest, best version of ourselves.

This, of course, applies to dealing with our pre-tax problems, as well. No one wants to pay taxes. But when you've saved money in a pre-tax account, that is the bargain, the deal, you made with the government… to pay the tax later.

No one likes when 'later' finally comes. It is a struggle. It seems painful, but in the end, it is the best thing we can do to come into our ultimate financial destiny.

If you already have a great deal of your money in pre-tax vehicles, there are strategies that can be implemented to reposition the wealth and control the tax.

The goal is, whatever your situation, to make paying the tax hurt as little as possible. Reposition your wealth to control the payment of your taxes to the extent legally possible. And the sooner you do it, the more control you will have.

The discomfort of paying the tax is inevitable, but that is the deal you made.

Like a space shuttle re-entering the Earth's atmosphere, there's no way it can re-enter without burning up. But NASA figured out how to save the space shuttle by *controlling the burn.* They figured out a way to bring the shuttle safely back to Earth.

Money in pre-tax accounts *will* be subjected to taxes, and it will hurt to pay the tax, but with strategic planning, that burn can also be controlled.

And there is something *special* about Retirement. It is the only time period of your life that YOU get to decide what tax bracket you will be in. You have the opportunity to reposition your accumulated pre-tax wealth into tax-free assets and permanently reduce your future taxes, simply by settling your bill with the government and paying your tax now. But when you leave it up to the government to tell you what you will owe in taxes, when you leave your wealth and financial legacy in pre-tax accounts, then you allow your future tax bill to be based on the government's future needs — you have given up control.

Understanding how taxes affect your wealth is imperative. So many of us are wooed by instant gratification from tax breaks we can see *today,* that we aren't thinking about our future selves; we aren't thinking about how taxes will affect us down the road.

No matter which way you swing it, no matter how much you end up forking over, paying taxes hurts.

But if you reposition your wealth to control the tax burn, instead of a wasp sting, all you'll feel is a little pinch.

When you take control of your taxes, you take back control of your wealth and your financial future.

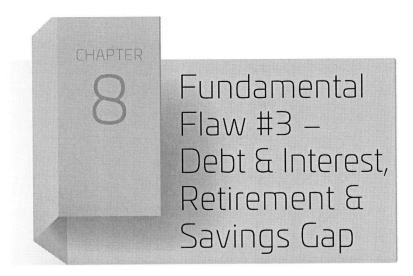

CHAPTER 8

Fundamental Flaw #3 – Debt & Interest, Retirement & Savings Gap

The Great Depression

My grandfather lived during the Great Depression.

When I was growing up, I was lucky to see him often. He was a big part of my life.

I'm sure that every grandfather is unique in his own right, but mine was especially distinct. Every time he came over, he brought a little plastic baggie filled with Grape-Nuts cereal.

In fact, he took the Grape-Nuts baggie with him everywhere. He wouldn't leave home without them!

When I was little, I thought it was kind of strange, and figured he just really loved Grape-Nuts.

It wasn't until I was older that my mother explained the reason behind the Grape-Nuts. Like I mentioned earlier, my grandfather lived during the Great Depression. At the time, Americans across the country were starving; they didn't know where their next meal was coming from.

Consequently, my grandfather was raised to conserve wherever and whenever possible. He was also learned to stockpile food for a rainy day. He carried around the baggie of Grape-Nuts cereal out of habit because his fear of hunger was second-nature.

I do not recall him ever actually eating the Grape-Nuts, but simply having them, just in case, gave him comfort and put him at ease.

Spending and Saving Habits

There is a fundamental problem with the way most of America saves today, and it's all because of instant gratification.

I, too, fall victim to the trap of instant gratification in American society.

Sometimes on my way into the office, I will place a Starbucks order on my smart phone so that by the time I get to the store, it will be waiting for me. (I know the coffee is pricey, so I don't indulge too frequently.)

I check my schedule for the day on my calendar app and squeeze in a virtual meeting with a client in another state using my video phone before I even get to the office.

When I travel, if I do not already have a car service lined up, I order an Uber as soon as the plane has landed so that I do not have to wait in the taxi line.

I order school uniforms online, and I pretty much do all my Christmas shopping via Amazon.

Our meals are delivered weekly via an organic food service so that we just have to prep and cook them.

Any spontaneous query I have can be immediately answered, wherever I am, thanks to the internet. I even have the full zillion page tax code and regulations manual on my cell in a tax law app!

It is not hard to see why waiting for anything in this day and age has become foreign, unfamiliar, and very uncomfortable. Delayed gratification is hardly a concept anymore. Saving for tomorrow, while expecting absolutely everything else now, now, now, has become a lost art.

Even through debt, we can still have whatever we want immediately — a lesson that has been taught best by our own country, America. With $20 trillion of acknowledged debt, multiple trillions more when adding in unfunded liabilities, America has now become the worst offender of living beyond its means, second only to China.

Our ancestors who lived through the Great Depression wouldn't recognize their country, its economy, or its people today. The shortages of the Great Depression have obviously long since been forgotten. We have gone from a culture of desperate savers to aggressive spenders, and the result is a country suffering from a massive Retirement Savings Gap (RSG).

Retirement Savings Gap

We've established that America has gotten conventional wealth building wrong for the last 35+ years.

Pensions have mostly disappeared and "Do-It-Yourself Pre-Tax Qualified Plans" have become our go-to retirement vehicles. We have become dependent upon these plans and the government, and as a result, we are completely unprepared for retirement as seen by the massive RSG.

What is the RSG exactly?

It's the difference between what a consortium of financial experts predicts Americans will need in retirement and what Americans actually have saved for retirement.

According to the National Institute on Retirement Security, for all U.S. households with inhabitants ranging in age from 25 to 64, the Retirement Savings Gap is projected to be between $7 and $14 trillion.[112] This means that of all adult pre-retirement households, we have under-supported and under-funded the lifestyle of our future selves by at least $7 trillion and at most $14 trillion. This is unfathomable!

Worse still, the World Economic Forum published a report in 2017 predicting that the world's RSG will be $400 trillion by 2050 and that underfunded government pension liabilities (AKA Social Security here in the U.S.) created this gap.[113] The article goes on to state that solutions include governments simply raising the 'target retirement age.' But how is that a solution? Not providing Social Security until a later age does not erase the gap for the individual. In fact, it makes it worse.

So, not only has America failed to save properly, we have also *grossly* overspent!

It becomes painfully obvious that most Americans are massively unprepared for retirement.

Suffer the Financial Consequences

Why is this happening? Why are most Americans unprepared for retirement?

When the 401(k) moved into wide acceptance in the 80s, and the company pension quietly retreated in our society, did any financial expert step up and publish any article, paper, or analysis to tell people how much they were taking upon their own shoulders? Did anyone tell them how much they would now need to put away on their own to replicate what was previously given to them outright? Did anyone tell them how much it would take to simply duplicate their company pension before accounting for the volatility of the investments they were placing this money in?

I can find no such publications, no such research, no such warnings anywhere. *None.*

Let's do the math. Assume that you make $100,000 annually.

Let's say that a pension would pay you 65 percent of what your highest salary was. All pensions are different. Some pay based on years of service, some pay based on the five highest earning years, and so on. They are all different, so we are just going to use a common average. So, without any adjustment for inflation, a single-life payout would be $65,000 (65 percent of $100,000).

This $65,000 is projected to be paid throughout your retirement for 30 years for a total payment of $1,950,000.

To calculate how much you would need to have in a market-based account like a 401(k), we run a Monte Carlo simulation. This simulation is a calculation of 5,000 possible scenarios all occurring simultaneously. These scenarios include a bull market, a bear market, a severe market correction, a severe market upswing, low interest rates, high interest rates, inflation, deflation, and so on. We run everything at the same time through regression analysis to give us a statistically reliable mathematical probability of success.

As you can see from the Monte Carlo simulation results in this chart, in order to take a $65,000 distribution per year for 30 years in retirement, we would need to accumulate $1,550,000, throughout our working years, to have a mathematical probability of success at 90 percent (with a 60/40 stock/bond portfolio split).

Retirement Monte Carlo Analysis

How many years should your portfolio last?	**30** years
What is your portfolio balance today?	**$1,550,000**
How much do you spend from the portfolio each year?	**$65,000** 4.2% of the portfolio

How is your portfolio invested?

Stocks: **60%**   Bonds: **40%**   Cash: **0%**

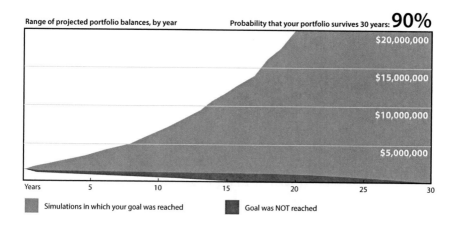

Range of projected portfolio balances, by year   Probability that your portfolio survives 30 years: **90%**

	$20,000,000
	$15,000,000
	$10,000,000
	$5,000,000

Years   5   10   15   20   25   30

■ Simulations in which your goal was reached   ■ Goal was NOT reached

Graph recreated from information provided by: Vanguard Group

But what do you need to save annually to accumulate this much? You cannot just divide $1.55 million by 30 working years, which would be $51,667 per year, because the portfolio value will grow over time due to compound interest or growth of the underlying capital, as in the case of the market.

So, we solve for the annual payment over various time periods, based on how many years out from retirement you begin to contribute. We have used a growth rate of 6 percent annually, which would itself be an issue because of the *New Normal* of extreme market volatility, but what we can clearly see in this chart is the sheer power of the time value of money.

Age	Years to Contribute	Annual Investment / Contribution
Age 25	40 Years	$10,015
Age 35	30 Years	$19,606
Age 45	20 Years	$42,136
Age 50	15 Years	$66,592

Assuming a growth rate of 6 percent annually, a 25-year-old needs to contribute a mere $10,000 per year where a 50-year-old, who has only 15 years left before retirement, must contribute $67,000 or 67 percent of their gross salary for the last 15 years before retirement – something that would be next to impossible.

It should be noted that in 2017, the maximum annual contribution into a 401(k) was capped at $18,000. Beyond the age of 50, if your plan allows it, you can contribute an additional $6,000 through the catch-up contribution, for a total contribution of $24,000. As you can see, these contribution limits only work with the annual contribution required of a 25-year-old but not for any other worker.

This means that if you are behind on your retirement contributions and are 30 or older, you *must* look at other options outside of a 401(k) in order to have even a *chance* of meeting your retirement goals. **This cannot be overstated or emphasized enough! It is simple math and math doesn't lie.**

From Saving to Spending

We also need to look at ourselves and see where we, as individuals, go wrong with building our wealth throughout our lives.

Besides what we are automatically putting aside for our future selves, it also really comes down to our spending habits.

An average American's spending habits look a little like this:[114]

> Day-to-Day Living Expenses: 40 percent
> Housing: 30 percent
> Transportation: 20 percent

That only leaves 10 percent for savings for the average American; only 10 percent for your future self! Your current self is winning, and, according to those numbers, the battle isn't even close.

If you look at the example above, 10 percent of $100,000 is $10,000, and that level of savings is *only* adequate for the 25-year-old's contribution requirements. It is a pretty safe bet that most 25-year-olds are not earning $100,000 either.

All the American households that have not put enough aside for their future selves have effectively contributed to the RSG. From the vast size of our retirement gap, at a minimum of $7 trillion, America's obsession with instant gratification has won far too many times over our future.

But one day the future will arrive and become the present. One day, your future self is going to wake up and realize much too late that they were cheated, swindled, and forgotten by the younger, less-wise version of themselves. Now they will be forced to suffer the financial consequences for the rest of their lives.

I am afraid it is true: *you are your own worst financial enemy.* Your younger self is sabotaging the security of your own financial future.

This is a conversation the entire country must have with themselves before it's too late.

10 Percent Isn't Enough

Right now, it isn't too late to take control of your finances. It isn't too late to start closing your personal RSG.

And you can start by figuring out how you will be able to put aside more than 10 percent.

It may seem like a lot of money in the short term, but 10 percent of your income simply isn't enough if you want to maintain your current lifestyle in retirement.

Think about it. Most Americans currently spend 90 percent of their income on living expenses. If we aren't happy unless we're spending 90 percent of our income on our lifestyle, what makes us think 10 percent will be enough once we retire?

Most financial advisors focus heavily on the 10 percent savings pot. They assume the other 90 percent of your income is already tied up, so they don't coach you to invest or save anything more than that.

But if we already know that 10 percent alone leads to failure, why would we plan around that?

America's entire wealth building engine is based on a 10 percent savings bucket, but it's really the bigger bucket we're missing the boat on. People in the know understand that building true wealth doesn't happen by saving a mere 10 percent of your income. People in the know understand that true wealth is built through compound interest accumulating over a lifetime.

Facing the Unknown

Let's take a quick look at an individual retirement savings gap simulation below:

Current Plan	Current Account Value	Annual Payment	Projected Growth Rate (net of fees)	Years until Retirement	Projected Nest Egg at Retirement	Withdrawal Rate	Pre Tax Income	Taxable	After Tax Cash Flow
IRA	$	$7,500	6%	30	$592,936	4%	$23,717	yes	$17,788
IRA	$	$	%		$0	%	$0	no	$0
IRA	$	$	%		$0	%	$0	yes	$0
Social Security							$27,000		$23,625
Total							$50,717		$41,413
Estimated Cash Flow									$41,413

If someone earning $75,000 per year saves 10 percent for 30 years at a 6 percent growth rate, he or she will end up with a nest egg of $592,936.

That doesn't sound like a whole lot, does it? Well, that's because it isn't.

At a 4 percent withdrawal rate, their pre-tax annual retirement income will be $23,717. After taxes, that's $17,788 a year. That's insanely low!

According to the experts, an annual retirement income of $17,788 a year would leave this person with a $-58,587 annual retirement cash flow gap.

$-58,587
Retirement Cash Flow Gap

That's not just impossible, that's unlivable.

Besides, saving just 10 percent doesn't make any sense. How can anyone expect to live for 30 to 40 years off 10 percent of what you earned and lived off of for the 40 years before that?

When factoring in market volatility, taxes and inflation, if you are determined to maintain your lifestyle, your current self and your future self should probably be splitting that dollar down the middle, 50-50.

Yes, your future self has compound interest on his or her side, but that can easily be offset by future tax rate increases and future inflation.

Think back to all the things we have been discussing in this book: the marshmallow study regarding instant gratification and how good things do come to those who wait.

Think about the 100 people from the beginning of the book. Out of those 100 people, which person are you? Are you one of the four that will actually achieve financial prosperity in retirement?

Unless you are one of the very few special ones, some sacrifices must be made by your current self in favor of your future self. Would you rather face the unknown? Would you rather take the risk now and hope you don't end up stressed about money when you're no longer able to work?

Or would you rather take control?

How Much Should You Be Saving?

I think we've established that saving 10 percent of your income isn't enough for building true wealth or saving for retirement.

But how much *is* enough?

That really depends on how old you are.

Take a look at this chart:

Age	Years to Contribute	Annual Investment / Contribution
Age 25	40 Years	$10,015
Age 35	30 Years	$19,606
Age 45	20 Years	$42,136
Age 50	15 Years	$66,592

If these annual investment/contribution amounts seem impossible to you, then you need to consider alternatives to growing your wealth. You need to consider options that will produce the cash flow you're looking for in retirement.

What does that number look like for you?

For most of us, distributions of 3 to 5 percent aren't going to produce the lifestyle you want from your cash flow.

So what happens if instead of living off 3 percent to 4 percent, you had an asset that could produce 8 percent to 9 percent?

That would change everything, right?

Now, a 35-year-old, instead of having to save $19,606 annually, can still achieve $65,000 after tax cash flow by saving just $8,100 each year!

We'll go into this in more depth in Chapter 11 where we discuss wealth building options.

**Pease note: This chart reflects the value of 2017 dollars and assumes a return of 6 percent each year. It does not account, in any capacity, for inflation.

A Hidden Tax

Inflation is something else to consider when thinking about building wealth and retirement savings.

Most Americans don't understand inflation or even know what it is. The concept is vastly misunderstood. Many think inflation is simply an increase in prices, but it's more complicated than that.

> "Inflation is the rate at which the general level of prices
> for goods and services is rising and, consequently, the
> purchasing power of currency is falling."[115]

Plainly put, it's an increase in the general price level. Not specific goods or services, but the aggregate cost of everything, overall.

Sometimes this occurs when production costs like wages and materials increase rapidly. Other times, it occurs when the demand for goods and services outweighs production capacity, like money-printing, for example.[116]

Because the government ultimately controls the amount of money printed each month, they *partially* control the rate of inflation.

We have no idea how much money the government is going to print, just like we have no idea how much the rate of inflation will increase between now and when we retire.

This makes inflation a hidden tax. Everyone should be aware of it and account for its effect in their long-term plan.

Both End Up at the Zero Line

Some Americans don't have any debt. For most Americans, that sounds crazy. But it's true.

There are still some people that buy only what they can afford. They save and when they have enough money saved up, they buy. There are many financial books dedicated to the subject of getting out of debt and how you should only buy what you can afford.

But unfortunately, saving like that misses the boat, too.

Savers and debtors are really the same, just in the reverse order.

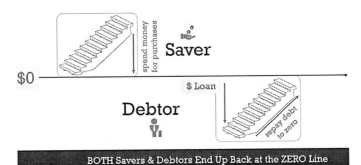

BOTH Savers & Debtors End Up Back at the ZERO Line

The saver saves up slowly, like steps on a ladder, until they have enough for their purchase. When they make their purchase, they deplete their account, taking them back to zero dollars.

The debtor does the exact same thing, only in the reverse order on the other side of the zero line. He or she acquires the money in a lump sum like a loan, and then pays it off incrementally over time. He or she slowly ascends the ladder back towards the zero line.

Undoubtedly, debtors and savers are on opposite sides of the financial spectrum, but they both end up in the middle, back at the zero line.

I know what you are thinking, "Yes, *but the debtor is paying interest and the saver is not.*"

Actually, both parties pay interest.

The debtor pays obvious interest costs to the money lender, whereas the saver pays interest in the form of opportunity costs. By spending the money, the saver loses out on the opportunity to invest that dollar for the rest of their life, meaning they have lost the earned interest. The saver loses interest on every dollar spent and not kept saved, earning a return. That is interest they can never get back because that money is gone forever.

Not only did the saver lose out on the interest that dollar would have earned for the rest of their life, they are also losing out on the earnings that those earnings would have earned, otherwise known as the compound interest that would have been earned on the invested dollar.

Both savers and debtors lose, because at the end of the day, both end up back at the zero line.

Engineer Your Financial Future

Is your head spinning?

Here I am, telling you that both savers *and* debtors end up at the zero line. You're probably starting to give up hope!

But stay with me.

What if I told you there was an account that allowed you to access money but still earn interest on that money? There's a way to *save* those opportunity costs and make all those dollars — the ones you save *and* the ones you spend — work for you.

This chapter makes painfully obvious what we already knew to be true… that America has become too big for its own britches by living in the moment and leaving the future in someone else's hands.

But it is not someone else's problem. It is ours if we want to be one of the four out of 100 who successfully builds financial security before they retire. While the rest are not saving anywhere near enough, we, the four out of 100, *must do it differently*. We must take the road less traveled and run our own race. It's time to take control and engineer your financial future!

GOING FORWARD FROM HERE

Legal Maximization of Wealth

Penny Wise and Pound Foolish

There is an old British idiom that says "Don't be penny wise but pound foolish," and it applies to people and situations where they take great care to not spend a penny but, through their actions, they cost themselves a great deal more.

One day, a couple of years ago, two of my wealthiest clients, John and Phyllis, came to see me. They wanted to discuss their assets and, more specifically, their estate plan.

As I sat down, John pushed their documents across the table. Phyllis said, "This is what we've had for the past five years. Is it okay?"

I looked down and blinked twice. I couldn't believe what I was seeing.

The document I had in front of me wasn't even legal in our home state. I could tell instantly because there was only one witness when there must be two, and the testator's signature was not at the bottom of the document, as also required. They had not even met the minimum requirement to have this document considered to be a legally valid will.

"Is anything wrong?" asked John.

"Well, this document is not valid in Florida, for starters. Where did you get it?" I responded.

They looked at each other and paused. After what felt like several, awkward minutes, Phyllis finally turned to me and said, "One of those legal companies you can find online."

Then, I saw John give Phyllis a little nudge before she said, "But we saved a preview of the document and then typed it up ourselves. We didn't want to pay the fees."

I stared at them in disbelief. Instead of a lawyer, they used a do-it-yourself website to manage their assets in death. Not only that, they didn't even pay for the online services so, when they recreated the document themselves, they misplaced the signatures! These were two of my wealthiest financial clients, yet they didn't want to spend any money on their estate plan.

It's one thing if you need to create a rental agreement for a piece of property you want to rent out (which can also be problematic for liability reasons) or a quick, simple contract to sell something yourself. For those simple contracts, I can understand the idea behind using one of these online companies. But using them for the legal transfer of your assets or your wishes upon your death is unbelievably risky.

I recently made a wealth presentation to an audience filled solely with affluent women in which I discussed the unique needs of women in financial and legacy planning. Afterwards, I was hanging around for a bit and many women were coming up to me with questions or comments to discuss.

One woman came up and said, "Rebecca, we just recently moved to Florida, and we know that we need to redo our estate plan, but all of the firms want to charge me an arm and leg just to type up some forms." She continued, "What would you charge me? Should I just use an online website?"

Talk about insulting someone in less than five seconds! She basically asked if my services were cheap, and if they were not, asked if she should just use an online service. Was she really expecting me to betray the value of being a lawyer by telling her that she could easily replace our craft through her use of an online website?

It would be like going up to a doctor and telling them they are way too expensive. "Doctor, don't you think I should just go to WebMD and diagnose myself?"

I always find it so amazing when someone mentions to me, a lawyer, that legal documents are just templates that we change. I have thousands of examples of how lawyers are not just form deliverers. We listen, we hear, and we draft around the quagmire of legal hazards that could and will arise in your particular case that you, as a non-legal mind, do not even know are potential issues.

This was another example of the need for instant gratification in America now. Everything is commoditized, instantized, and computerized.

Why do we need an actual lawyer? The forms are online.

But really, you aren't paying for the forms, but for the legal expertise and protection from what can potentially go wrong within those forms. You are paying for the legal knowledge of how these circumstances have gone wrong a thousand times before you and how they were resolved in litigation so that your lawyer knows how to draft around those potential, future problems, all so that you do not end up with the wrong end of the short stick when an argument arises between parties. And please keep in mind that when you are not a lawyer, you do not know what you do not know, so you cannot possible think of all of the things that could or have gone wrong under similar circumstances – thus the profession of law.

So no, it is probably not a good idea to discount the meaning of your life's legal plan through the use of an online website.

Thank goodness John and Phyllis came to me when they did. We fixed their estate plan and created the right transfer documents before anything unexpected and tragic happened, ensuring their assets would be protected. The time and expense that would have been incurred trying to use their previous invalid documents would have needlessly cost their heirs big time.

In 2012, Everything Changed

When you don't have a will, a trust, or an estate plan in place, you stand to lose a lot more than the dollars you saved by not creating one! Thinking about it like that, doesn't saving that money seem quite silly? Your entire net worth is at stake – the security of your family and your desire to take care of them!

Even though the document my clients presented to me was not even remotely valid, at least they had the wherewithal to create one at all.

Many, many Americans do not believe they need a will or trust. Most Americans incorrectly believe that they do not have enough assets to warrant creating one.

The American Taxpayer Relief Act of 2012 changed many estate tax laws and provided an increased $5 million lifetime wealth transfer exemption to every American citizen and permanent green-card resident. If one American is married to another American, or permanent resident, then that amount can double to $10 million (if you elect something called 'portability'). These amounts are indexed for inflation annually, so the 2017 amounts are adjusted upwards to $5.49 million individually and $10.98 million jointly with portability.[117]

When this law increased the lifetime wealth transfer exemption, it affected a large number of Americans. Suddenly a couple could pass $10 million down to their heirs, estate-tax free!

So, what's the problem?

Well, just because you do not have to pay an estate tax does not mean that you do not need an estate plan directing the legal disposition of your assets. People have confused the two, but not owing a tax has nothing to do with distributing your assets at your death.

Why You Need an Estate Plan

This is obviously not a book about estate planning. That is a book unto itself. This is a book about protecting and maximizing your wealth, and of course, that includes legally protecting it and transferring it the way you desire!

Even if the federal estate tax exemption applied to over 99 percent of all Americans, those Americans that own real property like a personal residence or rental property, those that own an automobile, those that have a bank account, those that have investment accounts, those that have any ownership in a partnership, an LLC, or a corporation, those Americans still need an estate plan.

If you have *any* assets of *any* kind, you need an estate plan! That may include just a will, a trust, or a combination of the two with a few additional basic documents. Whatever the appropriate design is for your situation, you need something in place to ensure that your wealth is transferred according to your wishes in as tax-efficient a manner as possible.

If you don't, your heirs may end up owing taxes on assets that are held up in probate (more on this later). They may even have to liquidate physical assets to cover those fees.

Estate planning is crucial to effectively and efficiently transfer your wealth and solidify your legacy.

It really all comes back to control. Who do you want to control your assets, your wealth, and your legacy?

Do you want it to be the government? Do you want it to be a team of lawyers you've never met who have little to no interest in your family's well-being?

Simply creating an estate plan can bypass all of that.

Trusts Are for Everyone... Really!

The high limits on estate taxes that were created in 2012 really created quite a problem. When people discovered they no longer needed to worry about an estate tax, they incorrectly believed that meant that they didn't need to have an estate plan. They did not (and still don't) realize the difference between not being charged an estate tax and having a legal plan in place to handle the disposition of your assets.

Like estate plans, most Americans also incorrectly assume trusts are only for the wealthy and elite. But that misses their purpose.

If you and your spouse are American citizens or permanent residents who jointly own a house, when one spouse dies, the other spouse inherits the house. This is typical in most states.

But who gets the house when the second spouse dies?

Unless you've already lived through it, you cannot begin to imagine how long and frustrating the legalities of the probate process can take. You have to hire lawyers, file paperwork, wait for the government to respond, and so on.

Creating a trust that owns the assets simplifies everything.

If you want your house sold and the proceeds split three ways, for instance, you would need to create a trust that explains such.

If you want to give the house to your favorite grandchild later in their life, only conditionally (say only if they graduated from college), you'd need to create a trust outlining those conditions.

Five Basic Legal Documents Everyone Should Have

When it comes to their assets, most Americans are not legally prepared for the unknown.

As a result, we're seeing more and more people dying without a will or any legal estate documents in place. People are dying intestate, that is, they pass away without any documents that legally control their wealth and asset transfers.

When you die intestate, your assets go through your state government and are distributed by the state's laws of intestacy, meaning they go to your heirs eventually, according to state law. This is called intestate succession.

Therefore, if you don't have a will in place when you die, the state government is going to dispose of your assets according to the state's legal scheme.

I would be remiss if I didn't talk, at least briefly, about the five legal documents needed for basic estate planning since the legal transfer of wealth is a large part of creating and maximizing your legacy.

What's the Difference Between a Will and a Trust

In this chapter, I've mentioned both wills and trusts, but I want to take a moment to differentiate between the two.

Most Americans have heard of both a will and a trust, but, as we have discussed, many people incorrectly believe that they do not have enough wealth to justify a trust.

If you have even a single asset you should have a will. If you want to avoid probating that will through the state court system, you should also create a trust because a trust is the main alternative to a will.

A will by itself has no legal effect when it is written, as it can be changed at any time all the way up until death or incapacity. It only becomes effective when the subject of the will, the testator, dies. Then, the will is given legal effect through a court process called probate. If an estate is insolvent or minor, there may be summary administration or no administration at all but this is beyond the scope of this book.

There are aspects of the probate process that most people find uncomfortable. First, the probate process is public. That means that anyone can access court documents that enumerate all of your assets. And it is a government process, making it technical and time consuming. In my experience, outside of a summary administration, it is rare that the process takes less than a year. And time means money — money that your heirs do not need to waste. The probate process can be quite a nightmare.

Everyone must *at least* have a will. But a trust is much more efficient. The idea is that the trust handles everything from the estate, and the will just acts as a catch-all for any asset that might have been inadvertently left out of the trust.

A revocable, or *inter vivos*, trust is a **living document**. It is continually updated and edited, creating a separate legal entity while you're alive. Once a trust is created, assets can be legally transferred immediately during your life, instead of just upon your death, as is the case with a will. Irrevocable trusts created during life are also an important wealth transfer and planning tool but are beyond the scope of this book.

This means that when you die with a trust, nothing legally changes as far as your assets are concerned. You have already legally handled the asset transfers during your life so that everything you'd want to happen after your death has effectively already happened. Your heirs will skip the probate process completely, unless any assets were missed and not transferred to the trust during your lifetime. Some assets pass outside of both a will and a trust via contract law, like those assets that have a beneficiary designation or a pay-on-death or transfer-on-death directive.

From a tax perspective, the IRS views a revocable trust the same as the grantor until death, so the trust creator will include trust assets' income and losses on their personal return.

Two Power of Attorneys

Having the legal documents in place to manage the legal transfer of your assets upon death are crucial.

But what about if you are injured but you *don't* die?

A **durable power of attorney (DPOA)** mitigates unexpected risk by giving someone else the legal power to act on your behalf. With a DPOA, you explicitly list each power you wish to convey to your agent to execute on your behalf. There are also limited powers of attorney that are restricted to conveying one or a few specific powers only. An example would be a limited power of attorney to execute the closing documents of a home sale, on your behalf, while you are out of the country.

A **medical power of attorney** gives your appointed agent the legal right to make medical decisions on your behalf when you are physically or mentally incapacitated.

An Advance Directive/Living Will

The last of the five documents is called an Advance Directive, or a **living will**.

A living will is similar to a medical power of attorney, except that the document itself spells out your wishes in certain medical circumstances instead of your POA agent deciding what should happen in medical situations where you are no longer able to convey your wishes directly, due to an illness or incapacity. There can be an overlap between your medical power of attorney and your advance directive, so the documents will state which holds authority over the other in the event of a conflict.

If you've ever had surgery, you were likely asked if you have a living will. If something goes wrong during the procedure, this is the document that the medical facility will turn to in order to execute your wishes.

For example, if something went wrong during a surgery and you slipped into a coma, would you want the doctors, nurses, and medical staff to do everything in their power to revive you?

Or would you rather they follow DNR (the Do Not Resuscitate option)?

Either way, an advance directive ensures that your wishes are known and adhered to in the event of a medical emergency.

You Have a Basic Responsibility

Unfortunately, there are a lot of Americans who do not have a basic will or trust or estate documents in place.

Maybe they are young and have not thought about it. Or maybe they think they do not have enough wealth to warrant a legal, asset transfer document.

Whatever the reason, if you don't have a will or a trust in place, you could stand to lose a large portion of your wealth and cost your family a great deal of time and aggravation when they are already dealing with the emotional difficulty of losing you.

And you most certainly will lose control. Should you die intestate, you have absolutely no say anymore over your own assets. The government will make those decisions for you and do with your assets what they may, all while charging your estate administrative costs and fees because running the government costs money. Is that something you really want?

You have a basic responsibility to yourself and your family to prepare a basic estate plan whether you think you need to or not.

President Trump proposed tax reform in 2017, which included the elimination of the estate tax, so several clients called and asked if they still need their estate plan. In response, I asked them three simple questions: 1. Has the estate tax been repealed before – YES, 2. Was it reinstated later on – YES, and 3. Will our government need more or less tax revenues in the future – MORE. Then I tell them that they need to answer their own question. It is probably not a good idea to unwind planning that very likely will continue to be necessary.

Let me end here by giving you one example.

Thanks to that law that we have been discussing throughout this chapter, most *married* Americans will be able to transfer approximately $11 million combined ($5.49 million each in 2017), estate tax free. However, once you have an estate value that surpasses that exclusion amount, the estate tax is applied at a flat 40 percent. So, if a family has $12 million in assets and the second spouse dies in 2017 and the family has utilized no estate tax planning other than portability, the family would owe an estate tax of about $400,000 as follows:

> Total Lifetime Exclusion Amount: $5,490,000 +
> $5,490,000 = $10,980,000
> Total Assets: $12,000,000
> Total Exclusion: $12,000,000 - $10,980,000 =
> $1,020,000 Taxable
> **40 percent of $1,020,000 = $408,000 owed in**
> **ESTATE TAXES**

But only if they've elected **portability**.

Portability allows the first spouse to transfer their unused lifetime exclusion (up to $5.49 million in 2017) to the surviving spouse at death, if the surviving spouse is a citizen or permanent resident. Because the first spouse can pass all of their assets to their surviving spouse (if the surviving spouse is an American citizen as different rules apply to residents and non-citizens) using the unlimited marital deduction, they do not use up any of their individual $5.49 million lifetime exclusion amount. Portability basically combines both spouse's lifetime exclusion amounts together, allowing the surviving spouse to pass down the entire $10.98 million in assets, estate-tax free, upon his or her death.

But portability is not given to you automatically. You have to file for it. In other words, it is an affirmative election made on the Estate Tax Return, Form 706, which must be filed even if there is no estate tax due. If you don't elect portability, you would lose the deceased spouse's unused lifetime exclusion amount.

Take our previous example above. Without filing a 706 to elect portability:

> Total Assets: $12,000,000
> Total Exclusion: $12,000,000 - $5,490,000 (only one
> spouse's exclusion amount) = $6,510,000 Taxable
> **40% of $6,510,000 = $2,604,000 owed in**
> **ESTATE TAXES**

Not electing portability costs this family $2,196,000 – their payment of $2.604 million less the $408,000 they would have paid by electing portability!

There have been so many Americans that have missed filing this election and were then forced to request relief through a private letter ruling from the IRS. The IRS was so inundated by these requests for relief that they created a new revenue procedure in June 2017, Rev Proc 2017-34, that now gives executors up to two years to affirmatively elect portability after the death of the first spouse.

But, is that a risk you really want to take? Are you willing to subject your spouse to potentially large losses in tax free assets, simply because you did not direct your appointed agent to file some paperwork?

We are talking about filing one piece of paper that is essentially worth $2,196,000 (40 percent of $5,490,000 in 2017)!

Taking this legal responsibility seriously, especially when you are married or have children, is crucial. Establishing a will, possibly a trust, both medical and durable powers of attorney, and an advance directive/living will and making sure that all of your beneficiary designations are up to date ensures the effective legal transfer of your assets at a basic level, according to your wishes.

Advanced planning of tax efficient wealth transfers beyond a basic estate plan will ensure the security of your wealth for decades to come.

Wealth Building Assets

Guess Who

One day, I was watching my son and my daughter play an old-time game, popular in the 80s and brought back as a classic in 2016, called *Guess Who*. In the game, the players sit opposite each other and each picks a main character from their separate stack of 24 character cards.

The object of the game is to be the first to guess the other player's main character. To do so, you only ask yes or no questions to eliminate characters.

You can ask if your opponent's main character has blonde hair, has a big nose, wears glasses, and so on.

Slowly, the options are dwindled down to reveal the answer.

Watching this simple game made me realize that, when choosing the right way to build wealth, a simple game of *'Guess What'* should be played.

We need to decidedly eliminate options that do not match our chosen result: building wealth in the most favorable container, the most favorable asset classes.

Guess What

How straightforward and easy might it be for people to eliminate options that do not meet their needs?

For example:

- If you are close to retirement and out of time to make-up for large market corrections, you should *eliminate* a 100 percent market-based portfolio because it has no built-in downside protection.
- If you want to control and reduce taxes, you should *eliminate* your pre-tax account, because future taxes are likely to increase dramatically, and there is no ability to control that tax once you are in retirement and tax rates have gone up.
- If you want a legacy option where you have control over distribution beyond death, you should *eliminate* any plan to **stretch your IRA** because your beneficiaries can elect to cash it out in a lump sum and spend it however they'd like, immediately.
- If you want long-term care (LTC) protection, you should *eliminate* all financial options that do not have LTC bolted on as an ancillary benefit.

Some Financial Advisors are Clueless

While this seems rather simple, the scary part is that many financial advisors have no idea what to eliminate.

Think about it.

When was the last time your advisor asked you to contemplate what the tax consequences will be for your children if they were to successfully "stretch" your IRA? Have they asked you to think about what the tax situation will look like in America some 25 years down the road?

Journal of Accountancy

I was recently interviewed by the Journal of Accountancy because I wrote an article on the upcoming largest transfer of wealth in the history of the world and how it has already begun, how large it will be, and how nothing before, including the Gilded Age, even comes close to the amount of wealth transferring down to the next generation.

In the article, I had stated that if someone were to inherit an IRA, they should consider paying the tax immediately over the next five years *instead* of following the standard advice to stretch it and avoid the tax for as long as possible (so that the RMDs, required minimum distributions, would be calculated on the heir's date of birth instead of the original owner's).

This one point caused the Journal to contact my publicist and request an interview. And let me tell you, it was quite an enjoyable one.

I explained to the Journal how I understood why the CPA's professional position is to maximize tax reductions and lower the tax due in the one singular year they were working on, but that as a wealth strategist and tax attorney, I was looking at the picture from the perspective of maximizing wealth and minimizing taxes over a client's lifetime, not just a single period.

I explained that from that perspective, and given the macroeconomic conditions of America in 2017, deferring taxes some 10 years or more no longer made sense, especially given that we will probably never again see our taxes as low as they are now. America, too, must pay the piper.

The Journal was very respectful even though what I said went completely against their ingrained philosophy. The interviewer simply said, "Oh my! You make me want to convert my IRA right away."

Now or Later

But really, let's think about this. If you inherit an IRA and you roll it over to your date of birth so that the required minimum distributions (RMDs) are due when you turn 70 1/2, it is likely that the account will grow considerably in value if you are years away from that birthday.

Let's say that you inherit $300,000 when you are 50 years old and you are right now in a 25 percent tax bracket because you are making $75,000 per year. If the account grows at 6 percent annually, by the time you are 70 and a half, your $300,000 will have grown to $990,584 (although keep volatility in mind).

Had you paid the tax over five years when you inherited it, you would have paid an effective rate of 20.2 percent because your income would have gone from $75,000 to $135,000. The additional tax would have been $15,912 per year, to convert $60,000 each year over the five years, to an after-tax bucket (assuming tax rates stay level for the five years).

	Current Income	Current Income + 20% Conversion
Taxable Income	$75,000	$135,000
Effective Tax %	15.10%	20.20%
Total Tax	$11,314	$27,226

But instead, you decided to forgo the tax and just let the money ride for 20 and a half years. Now, it is 2037, 20 years later. The last Baby Boomer retired seven years ago and tax rates have resultantly changed. Your account grew at 6 percent for 20 years, and your inherited IRA balance is now $990,584. Your RMD is $37,381, so you *must* take at least that amount out this year, at a minimum, and pay the tax on that distribution.

But, you want to replicate your income, so you take a distribution of $75,000 and you figure that the distribution in addition to your $24,000 Social Security (assuming it still exists and you are still entitled to receive it) gets you to your pre-retirement income level: the amount you were making just before you retired.

So, now we calculate the tax on this $75,000 IRA distribution and $24,000 in Social Security income. Your taxable income is $75,000 plus 85 percent of $24,000, which equals a total taxable income of $95,400. If tax rates increase only slightly by just 10 percent from their 2017 levels (a mere 10 percent increase is totally unrealistic given the government's funding requirements in 2030, thus there is an extremely high probability that the rates will go up much, much more than a mere 10 percent), the tax on the $95,400 would be $29,129. That's an effective tax of 30.5 percent, meaning your after tax income would be $69,871. That is quite a hefty tax bill for someone retired and on a fixed income.

The Worst Part — No Control

The worst part is that now that you are retired (remember, this is 20+ years into the future), taxes have already gone up 10 percent. We cannot rewind the clock and pay the tax back when you were 50, when you could have paid the tax at a 20 percent effective rate. Taxes are now higher, and every dollar you take out now in retirement will be taxed at that higher tax level.

But, it's actually worse than that. What if the government returned to the *average* 61 percent top marginal tax levels America has had for the last 100 years? This would increase this retiree's tax bill to over $50,000, reducing their net income to less than $49,000.

But what can this retiree do then?

Nothing. At this point, it is simply too late for tax strategy planning. They are retired, and their money is in a pre-tax account. If they are going to take that money out to live on, they are going to pay the tax at whatever the tax rate is at in the year that they take the distribution. The government is counting on this!

But what if I am wrong? What if tax rates remain the same for 20 years (although if you read the chapter on taxes, you know this is not really mathematically possible)? In this case, we now owe the same tax rate on $990,584, instead of on $300,000. So, now you are paying taxes on $690,584, on which you could have not paid one red cent. Thus, you are *still* paying more in taxes.

It is the difference between paying for the seed when you get it versus paying for the entire harvest that seed yields.

It's likely your financial advisor, like most financial advisors, is not thinking in those terms. Instead, they are thinking about maximizing your cash flow in the now — *more instant gratification.* They are planning for the current you — not for your future self. They may even think that you will be in a lower tax bracket in retirement thanks to conventional wisdom. But conventional wisdom in the area of tax deferral is wrong for America, version 2017.

Eliminate the Unnecessary

Most of our clients think as we do and see the need for a legacy minded solution that makes sense from both a growth/volatility perspective and a tax perspective. There is no sense in growing your pie if the government will just take larger and larger portions away. Additionally, they want a solution that allows them to maintain control beyond death, if desired. Being legacy minded means that you want to leave your family in a financially better position. This means that we need to look for the *best* way to transfer wealth to the family. We want to maximize wealth and minimize tax in the process.

Just like that game of Guess Who, we can work to define goals and eliminate options that simply will not support them.

Let's take a look at some options that may need to be eliminated.

Stretch IRAs

As our detailed example above illustrates, the entire premise of a stretch IRA is to defer payment of the taxes on that account for as long as possible, generations even. The heirs then pay the tax when they reach the **Required Minimum Distribution** (RMD) age. Currently, that is 70 1/2 years old.

The problem with stretch IRAs is that they provide literally no tax control. They are designed to grow the asset over that additional generation and pay the taxes as late as possible. If we were to successfully grow this vehicle to millions of dollars, what good would that be to our heirs if taxes return to their all-time highs of greater than 90 percent?

And if you still don't think a 90 percent or higher tax rate is possible, let me remind you that taxes have been as high as 94 percent in 1944 and have reached levels of 90 percent multiple times in our history!

Do not forget that, during the 50s, 60s, and 70s, until 1982, tax rates were 35 percent on an income of just $35,000. It has only been the last 30 years that America has been spoiled by low tax rates, which ironically coincides with the sharp rise in our national debt after the end of the gold standard. And while tax revenues were reduced, we vastly increased our spending. As a result of lower tax revenues and higher spending for the last three decades, we have lived more on credit and debt than on tax receipts.

Given that America is now in the worst fiscal position of its history, why shouldn't we expect taxes to increase dramatically? Why shouldn't we expect it to hit or surpass that 90 percent threshold? How much longer can we live on credit when our national debt has already surpassed $20 trillion? Debt that will grow even faster as the Boomers retire.

Not only should we expect much higher taxes in the future, we desperately need to plan for them. **True wealth building isn't just about growing the pie, but also very much about controlling how big of a slice the government decides to take in the future.**

In accounts like stretch IRAs, the government gets to decide every year how big that slice is. This leaves us and our heirs with zero control.

OPTION ELIMINATED!

100 Percent Market-Based Portfolios

The second option we need to consider eliminating is a 100 percent market-based portfolio.

How can we grow wealth uninterrupted year after year in this *New Normal* of large market increases followed by correspondingly large losses?

If we truly want to take advantage of the eighth wonder of the world – compound interest, uninterrupted over a generation – we cannot *solely* use a market-based portfolio or market-indexed product.

Because we know the market will always have some years of losses, and those years will interrupt our growth on the compound yield curve.

OPTION ELIMINATED!

Directly Inherited Accounts

Despite what you might think, directly inherited accounts aren't safe either.

If we want to be able to control the distribution of our wealth to our heirs beyond our death, we must eliminate *all* options where our heirs directly inherit the financial account at death.

This requires advanced legal planning because the assets are likely either owned outright with a named beneficiary, where the asset will be transferred directly upon death, or transferred directly by a will or a testamentary trust. We must therefore implement a trust so that the distribution parameters within the trust allow us to control the money even beyond our death.

OPTION ELIMINATED!

Uniform Transfer To Minors Act & Uniform Gift To Minors Act

Some clients have thought that it makes sense to use either the **Uniform Transfer to Minors Act** (UTMA) or the **Uniform Gift to Minors Act** (UGMA) to create accounts through which to transfer wealth.

Both used to be dependable ways to gift assets to grandchildren, but now they have no tax benefits. The accounts are taxable year after year from day one, and the Kiddie Tax rules have eliminated any positive tax differential that used to exist.

Furthermore, the gifts are irreversible and are given to the child outright to do with as they please at the age of maturity. Typically, depending on the state laws under which the account was established, the age of maturity is between 18 and 25 years old.

This obviously leaves us no tax benefits in the meantime and no control of any kind since the gifts are irrevocable and theirs outright at maturity.

OPTION ELIMINATED!

529 Plans

Lastly we turn to the **529 plan**.

These plans have become the go-to college planning tool and are quite common for this purpose. However, they really aren't intended to be legacy transfer mechanisms because their *singular focus* is to provide for college expenses.

The funds contributed to a 529 plan grow tax free and are taken out tax free *as long as* they are used towards 'qualified education expenses.' If they are not used for qualified expenses, not only is the account taxable as a regular investment, but there is also a 10 percent tax penalty for not using the funds for educational purposes.

Also, 529 plans offer extremely limited investment options state by state — even fewer than your 401(k) options — and investment allocations can only be modified once per year, similar to an open enrollment change period. If you want to change your investment allocations more than once in a year, you can only do so if you are also changing the beneficiary.

Another caveat exists in that you are only allowed to change the beneficiary to a sibling of the *original* beneficiary.

What happens if your child or grandchild decides to skip college altogether? Maybe they decide to join the military or the Peace Corps. Maybe they decide to develop an app or run a blog. Better yet, maybe they get a full ride to college and don't need the money.

If they don't have a sibling you can roll the account over to, you're at a loss and must pay the tax and the penalty to withdraw your own money. The tax advantages of 529s are severely restrictive.

But beyond that, there is something inherent in the design of a 529 Plan that I believe to be a glaring financial flaw. I am a true believer in the power of compound interest, but these 529 plans force the account holder to deplete the funds in the account roughly 18 years into its establishment — right when compound interest is working its magic.

And we continue to deplete it for the next three years until the account is drained to nothing. This action completely closes the account, eliminating any further growth potential.

Any financial account that must be used in its entirety within 22 years of its inception is *clearly* not a viable wealth building or wealth transfer tool. A 529 is a singularly focused, narrowly-tailored vehicle that exists for one purpose and one purpose only: to provide tax-free funds for education.

Most of my clients care about making an impact throughout their grandchild's entire life. They want to help with college, and they want to help with the wedding. They want to help with the first house, and they even want to help with retirement. If that's your goal, then putting all your eggs in this single purpose 529-basket is not the plan for you.

And if all of those reasons weren't enough to convince you of its unsuitability, 529s have one more financial flaw. They are 100 percent market participatory, making them subject to market volatility.

This flaw was really exposed in 2008 and 2009. Families that utilized a 529 plan as their sole source of college funding saw major losses during the Great Recession. Children that were scheduled to jet off to college shortly thereafter no longer had the funds to support them.

If you put your assets in a 529 plan and the market crashes right before your child packs their bags, there is no time to recover and recapture funds from those losses. In the crash of 2008, the S&P 500 took over four years to regain what it lost, which is the same amount of time as the average undergraduate education.

This makes using an exclusively market-based strategy for college funding incredibly risky. Children typically graduate from high school and attend college in a specifically defined time frame. And we have no way of controlling whether the market will be crashing or spiking during that time. This is the equivalent of a Sequence of Returns Risk for college instead of retirement – like we discussed in Chapter 6!

We need financial plans to perform when we need them to perform. We need to be able to control our wealth.

OPTION ELIMINATED!

The Roth

While a Roth does resolve our tax problems in the future, other problems exist that Roths don't resolve.

First, you cannot even contribute to a Roth if you earn too much income. You can do a back-door conversion, but that has its own issues.

The Roth is subject to market volatility because growth is market participatory through its market-based portfolio. A Roth has a five-year seasoning requirement before gains can be accessed. Further, gains cannot be accessed before age 59 1/2 or they are taxable, along with a 10 percent penalty.

Unlike other "tax-free" options, they also track a client's basis and report it annually to the IRS — an interesting requirement indeed for a tax-free account. Because of the market volatility, this option should be eliminated *as the sole, exclusive* wealth solution and should instead be leveraged alongside other tax-free assets.

The Most Tax-Advantaged Way to Grow Wealth

So, what remains uneliminated in our game of *Guess What?* We've discussed time and time again the importance of compound interest. Finding a tax-advantaged vehicle to help you consistently accumulate interest is crucial when building your wealth.

But even more specifically, wouldn't the best type of wealth building tool let you access money and still earn tax-advantaged interest on that money?

It would mitigate opportunity costs. More money in the bank means more compound interest working for you.

Remember the client I mentioned at the beginning of the book that turned $1.26 million into a future $45 million?

Well, I'm going to let you in on the solution.

My client grew those accounts using life insurance.

It may seem hard to believe, but it's true. Life insurance is the most tax-advantaged way to build true wealth and has been since our tax code was written over 100 years ago.

The Golden Child of the U.S. Tax Code

As a tax attorney, I have always looked to the tax code to unveil the most tax-advantaged asset class. It could be franchise restaurants, it could be car dealerships, it could be shipping containers, or even gold. Whatever the code states is the most tax-advantaged asset class, that is what we leverage for the benefit of clients. And the code unequivocally reveals that it is life insurance. It is the "Golden Child" of the tax code!

Life insurance is really the only asset class that, without restrictions, can grow tax-free, be accessed during life tax-free*, and be distributed at death tax-free*. And it's been like this for over 100 years.

It all started as a way to protect widows and their children. Women weren't legally allowed to work until 1920.[120] If their husbands died prematurely from disease, during battle, and so on, how would they be able to care for their children and for themselves?

Responsible husbands took out life insurance policies to ensure the safety of their families. Thus, the government decided not to tax these policies. They aren't being altruistic here. Life insurance is seen as society's private way, outside of the government, to provide for families. Therefore, the tax-free nature of these policies is justified. If these funds were taxable, their use would greatly diminish, and the government would be further saddled with the financial responsibility of caring for more of its citizens.

Tax-free distributions have to follow specific requirements, so you must work with an advisor who knows how to design and access these policies within specific parameters.

A Sophisticated Wealth Building Tool

What started out as a benefit for widows and their children, and remains so to this day, has also been leveraged as a sophisticated wealth building tool.

Originally, these policies were very expensive, but over time, life insurance companies started utilizing the tax-advantaged status to benefit all of their clients. Now, the average Joe could build wealth inside of a life insurance account, when structured correctly, and utilize all the lifetime benefits without tax implications.

Life insurance became an asset that was useful beyond the standard death benefit. The wealthy have been employing the lifetime benefits to build tax-advantaged wealth inside the policy for hundreds of years. Today, these policies are even more strategically designed to maximize these living benefits with money that can be accessed while the policy holder is still alive.

This progression is really quite logical. People with life insurance policies are paying premiums, so insurance companies realized it would be nice for these people to get something for their money while they're still alive by allowing them to save money within their policies.

Obviously, these types of policies provide insurance companies with additional revenue streams, but because those funds can be accessed whether you're alive or dead, the product becomes immensely valuable.

Common Misconceptions about Life Insurance

When most Americans think about life insurance, most equate it with a death benefit only.

This is a common misconception.

Term life insurance policies exist that solely provide death benefits, certainly. The premiums are very inexpensive, but they don't provide the policyholder with any living benefits. You're only covered if you die.

In fact, only 6 percent of all term policies actually pay a death benefit because they are designed to expire before your actual expected mortality age. Your term policy may seem cheap now, but price out a 20-year, $1 million dollar term policy on a 65-year-old or 70-year-old, and see how expensive they are!

No, in actuality, a term policy is only cheap during the period of your life in which there is an extremely low probability of death. The law of large numbers, which is what insurers base their actuarial science on, says that roughly three or four people out of 100 may die prematurely, but the 97 or so people that do not die (and who still pay their premiums) will make up for the few that *do* die unexpectedly and receive payouts. These numbers result in quite a large profit overall for any insurer.

A **permanent life insurance policy**, however, provides you with benefits during life because you can always access your cash. The premiums you're contributing are adding to your account's overall cash value after the cost of the insurance's death benefit.

Permanent life insurance policies are always more expensive because you are over-funding the policy beyond the cost of the death benefit.

This surplus cash builds and grows tax free within the insurance vehicle. These policies are leveraged to build wealth and the money you contribute into the pot grows and compounds and further makes money.

Many Americans are conventionally trained to buy term life policies and then invest their savings into the market – 'Buy Term and Invest the Difference' has become a famous tagline. But this book is meant to build a case proving how America has gotten building wealth and preparing for retirement entirely wrong. If this strategy worked, this book would not be possible.

Besides, as we have seen with America's RSG — retirement savings gap — America has bought term and SPENT the difference!

Utilizing a permanent life policy is a great way to force yourself to save.

Permanent Life Insurance is Commonplace

When I tell my clients about the tax benefits of permanent life insurance policies, they think they're too good to be true.

The immediate response is most often, "Why haven't I ever heard of this?"

Many Americans haven't heard about permanent life insurance because it has never been in their purview. Most Americans don't usually talk to financial advisors at my level unless they are paying or expect to pay extremely large income or estate taxes. The average American who doesn't have $10 million in assets doesn't necessarily talk to a tax lawyer. They don't even know permanent life insurance is an option for wealth building.

But now that you know this type of tool is available, you'll probably start to notice just how mainstream it is. You'll probably start to see examples of permanent life insurance policies being used everywhere.

In financially sophisticated circles, permanent life insurance is very commonplace. There are a ton of examples of titans of industry — including Walt Disney[121], JC Penney[122], and Conrad Hilton[123] — that used the cash in their life insurance account to achieve their dream or keep their dream going during a rough patch like the Great Depression.

What If the Laws Change?

I know what a lot of you are thinking...

"But what if the laws change? What if these permanent life insurance policies are suddenly taxed?"

The tax code has favored these types of policies for over 100 years, and in that time, the law has only changed once during President Reagan's 1986 Tax Reform Act.

The change required people to spread their premium payments going into the policy over a minimum number of years. They were no longer allowed to simply dump in one lump sum to fund the policy.

But even when that law changed, anyone with an existing policy was grandfathered. The change only impacted new policies issued going forward.[124]

While certainly no one can predict the future, it is quite logical that future changes would not apply to previously created policies, which were created under different laws.

All that being said, we really do not know what Congress will do, right?

Time and time again, taxing the cash value inside permanent life insurance policies has been proposed. But year after year, the proposals have been denied.

The wealthiest people and companies in our country use permanent life insurance policies to build and transfer wealth. In fact, they use them to secure collateralized notes, defer compensation, fund buy-sell agreements, you name it!

Every sophisticated financial transaction that you can possibly imagine usually involves some form of life insurance contract. The wealthiest of the wealthy leverage life insurance. It is a trillion-dollar industry.[125]

And when it comes to our government officials, it is highly likely that the ones "in the know" also have a lot of money in life insurance.

A vote to tax policies, to tax widows and children, and all the others too, seems a distant possibility...

The Wealthy Have Been Doing It for Years

The wealthiest Americans have been leveraging permanent life insurance to build wealth for over 100 years.

But this tool is a bit of a secret. Few Americans have heard about permanent life policies.

Take a big bank, for example. Most of us are familiar with their retail arm and the branch you commonly visit.

But what most of us don't know is that each of these banks that offer wealth management have a private level reserved for their wealthiest clients.

It is on these private levels that clients are introduced to permanent life insurance policies. In fact, many of these banks have employees that specialize in these types of wealth building tools.

But unless you meet a minimum financial requirement of typically upwards of $5 million in assets, you're never invited to the private bank level; you're never told about permanent life insurance as an option to build wealth.

It's America's best kept financial secret.

Magnitude of Life Insurance

In addition to building individual wealth, permanent life insurance policies are also used to build corporate wealth. In fact, corporate-owned life insurance and bank-owned life insurance, known as COLI and BOLI respectively, are special sub-insurance industries that are so large that banks themselves could say that they are in the insurance business.[126]

Furthermore, most business partnerships buy life insurance policies to enable the partnership to buy-out a partner's family in the event of a partner's death, retirement, divorce, bankruptcy, etc, using the policy's cash value to execute the buy-out if the event is other than death.

Permanent life insurance policies are funding all kinds of buy-sell partnerships and agreements in America.

The size and scope of the use of insurance as a financial asset in America and its impact on America's financial system simply cannot be overstated.

Protecting Wealth

My firm handles a lot of estate planning and asset transfers. When clients have an estate tax issue, we routinely use an irrevocable life insurance trust (ILIT). An ILIT protects that policy from being included as part of the estate and taxed like the rest of the estate. It's a way for the wealthy to both reduce their estate tax and fund the paying of the reduced estate tax, thus protecting their wealth and providing liquidity to pay the estate tax. Overall, it is a tremendous asset protector, especially for intergenerational wealth.

In all reality, in the wealth preservation and planning business (which heavily includes tax reduction and control), it is difficult to think of sophisticated transactions that do not involve a life insurance component.

It is also heavily favored and protected under state laws against the claims of creditors, judgments, and liens. For example, here is an excerpt of Florida Statute §222.14 protecting the cash value of life insurance and annuities from all creditors:

The 2017 Florida Statutes

Title XV HOMESTEAD AND EXEMPTIONS	Chapter 222 METHOD OF SETTING APART HOMESTEAD AND EXEMPTIONS	View Entire Chapter

222.14 **Exemption of cash surrender value of life insurance policies and annuity contracts from legal process.**—The cash surrender values of life insurance policies issued upon the lives of citizens or residents of the state and the proceeds of annuity contracts issued to citizens or residents of the state, upon whatever form, shall not in any case be liable to attachment, garnishment or legal process in favor of any creditor of the person whose life is so insured or of any creditor of the person who is the beneficiary of such annuity contract, unless the insurance policy or annuity contract was effected for the benefit of such creditor.

History.—s. 1, ch. 10154, 1925; CGL 7066; s. 1, ch. 78-76.

Why Not You?

This is what the wealthy are doing to build their legacies through the generations and you can, too. Most of America is using the 401(k) as their primary wealth building tool, while the wealthy are leveraging the power of uninterrupted compound interest and tax-free wealth accumulation through the most tax-advantaged asset class under the tax code.

Which do you think is the superior vehicle?

Complicated and Misunderstood

But you need to be careful. Many financial advisors will tell you that life insurance is too expensive, doesn't grow like the market, or even that it is kind of a risk. Why?

Structuring these policies to benefit you is complicated and, quite honestly, not as lucrative as other, more common investment options. Many financial advisors negate permanent life insurance policies for their clients simply because they, as consultants, won't make as much money, or, more often, because it is outside the scope of their market-based world.

In addition, most financial advisors look at life insurance only as something that requires need-based analysis to protect against premature death only. That is the sanctioned financial stance on life insurance policies from the investment community.

Because of that, many market-based financial advisors only think within the confines of the three corners of the market. I call these advisors 'triangle advisors.'

The market triangle has stocks/equities in corner one, bonds/debt in corner two, and some variant thereof like mutual funds, index funds, or ETFs in corner three. But our practice follows a more diversified asset approach to building a secure and stable financial house, as shown in this image. As you can see, there is a proper place in an appropriately designed financial house for market based positions, but a safe and solid foundation must also be established, especially once a client is within 10 years or less of retirement. Having your assets 100 percent market based results in a top-heavy non-diversified financial house. This is why the ROTH, alone, cannot be our sole financial vehicle.

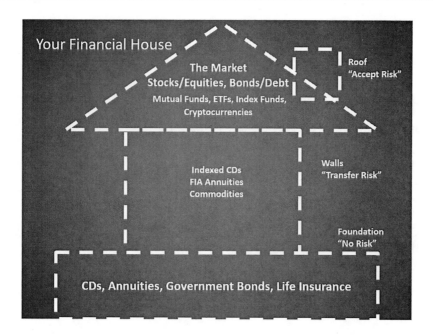

Triangle advisors don't really understand permanent life insurance. Their perspective on asset diversification is to spread wealth across variations of equity or debt asset classes — large-cap, mid-cap, small-cap, international, emerging-market, dividend paying, non-dividend growth, short-term, long-term, AAA, BB, etc. — all of which remain within those three market corners. They don't understand diversification between various asset classes including real estate, life insurance, and other non-equity, non-debt investment options.

Permanent life insurance policies are sophisticated and complicated and can certainly be very misunderstood. When considering this as a strategy, always work with an insurance and tax expert that specializes in leveraging the use of life insurance for wealth building purposes.

CHAPTER

11

Building
Your Legacy

Two Effective Ways to Maximize Wealth

In our experience, there are two effective ways to use the cash value of a permanent life insurance policy.

The first is an **Indexed Universal Life** (IUL) policy. It uses an indexing strategy to build wealth. The second is a **Whole Life** policy, which boasts a steadier, more conservative approach.

Before we move forward, I want to make sure to mention a third permanent life insurance policy option: **variable universal life** (VUL). These options exist, but the policies integrate the volatility of the market into a life insurance policy, meaning that you can lose money within these policies due to a decline in the market.

I believe in total transparency with my clients and want to make sure information is presented in totality. However, because these VUL policies bring the volatility of the market into the insurance vehicle, my practice does not present this option as a viable method for wealth building. Remember, our goal is to sufficiently resolve the two biggest threats to building wealth successfully — market volatility and taxes — which eliminates the use of any type of VUL. Another *Guess What* option gone.

Instead, we maintain a market position through the use of a ROTH while balancing that volatility risk with the use of IUL or traditional Whole Life policies that are not subject to the risk of loss through market volatility and thus, they never lose money due to a market downturn. Since they are both life policies, there are still insurance charges during downturn years to be aware of, but they both feature the tax benefits of being the Golden Child of the U.S. tax code.

Indexed Universal Life

Warren Buffet's #1 Rule to building wealth is: "Never lose money."

So, how do you grow wealth without losing money? More specifically, how do you growth wealth *rapidly* without losing money?

According to Buffett himself the best way is found through S&P 500 low-cost **indexed funds**.[127]

An index fund's performance is based on the underlying stocks' performances that make up that index, much like how the growth in a mutual fund is based off the growth of the individual stocks within that fund. When the market as a whole goes down, the index will also go down. In other words, you can lose money in an index fund.

But Indexed Universal Life policies (IULs) do not directly buy index funds. Instead, they utilize options on indexed funds to grow the cash value without the risk of loss in the most tax-advantaged way possible within the policy.

When you pay your premium, a portion of that money supports the death benefit within the policy and the balance goes into a general account, which is managed by the insurance company. The company then uses that money to buy options on the index.

Options are typically purchased from the S&P 500, but can be purchased from *any* index. When the market performs, the options get exercised and the returns from the index get credited to your IUL.

Buying options on an index costs money. So, options are bought up to a certain percentage of growth in order to manage their costs.

There are uncapped options, but typically the expense is cost-prohibitive. Thus, for maximum cost-efficiency, these options are usually purchased with a growth cap averaging between 10 and 13 percent. If you are thinking that you are missing out on the growth above these caps, keep a few things in mind: 1st — you continue to maintain a market based position in your balanced and diversified portfolio, and 2nd — when the IUL eliminates losses through the use of options, it is not necessary to have growth above these caps since we never lost principal during market declines. If you look back at the market since the 1900s, you will notice that most of the excessive growth years follow the extraordinary market decline years.

And the best part is that if the market goes down or even crashes, the options simply expire, unused. You do not lose any money because you were never directly invested in the market!

You are always hoping the market performs well and the options are exercised, but in the event that the market doesn't perform, your money is protected.

This is exactly the type of growth using indexes that Warren Buffett was talking about, except that it also follows his #1 Rule to 'Never Lose Money.'

And because we know the Bear, an overall downward market correction of 20 percent or greater, will always come, especially following years of solid, consecutive growth, this is like having our cake and eating it, too!

Getting Better All the Time

Many life insurance policies are built to maximize the death benefit, but my practice designs IULs to *maximize your wealth.*

And the policies' designs keep getting better.

Similar to the way we upgrade our smart phones every other year, IULs have become increasingly advanced and more diverse. As previously mentioned, there are now strategies that present no limit or cap on upside growth, but at a much greater cost of course. There are also policies that are created specifically to reduce the expenses in the later years of the policy to keep the cash value growing at the highest rate possible.

When I sit down with clients and show them the potential cash value growth of these policies, they are quite surprised and excited that they can grow their money without all the worry.

This is exactly why working with an expert is crucial, and why you can't just turn to the internet to replicate these highly specialized services. There are different policies for different cash needs, wealth building, and retirement goals.

If you don't work with an expert, your chances of achieving retirement success are greatly diminished should the wrong policy decision be made. When we leverage the use of a properly structured IUL, balanced with a continued market based strategy, among other assets, we have built an appropriately constructed financial house.

You could really setback your chances for wealth building success if you choose the wrong advisor.

Maximizing Retirement Cash Flow – An Example

Remember back to Chapter 8 where we discussed the Retirement Savings Gap. We introduced a chart of what people of different ages would need to contribute to a 60/40 Stock/Bond portfolio in order to accumulate enough money to have a 90 percent probability of taking a $65,000 distribution per year in retirement for 30 years.

Age	Years to Contribute	Annual Investment / Contribution
Age 25	40 Years	$10,015
Age 35	30 Years	$19,606
Age 45	20 Years	$42,136
Age 50	15 Years	$66,592

Because an IUL is not exposed to the risk of loss and because the proceeds are distributed tax-free (when structured properly), you could actually fund less into the IUL as compared to a traditional market portfolio (based on average market growth of around 6.29 percent per year when losses are eliminated and growth is capped); that's the beauty of this policy type! In this new chart below, you can see that a 25-year-old only needs to contribute $3,850 to an IUL policy for 30 years to receive a projected $65,000 per year for 30 years; a 35-year-old needs to contribute $8,100 for 25 years; a 45-year-old needs to contribute $19,250 for 20 years; a 50-year-old needs to contribute $32,400 for 15 years; and even a 55-year-old could contribute $64,000 for only 10 years to get a projected $65,000 cash flow in retirement for 30 years.

USING IUL VEHICLE		
Age	**Years to Contribute**	**Annual Investment / Contribution**
Age 25	30 Years	$3,850
Age 35	25 Years	$8,100
Age 45	20 Years	$19,250
Age 50	15 Years	$32,400
Age 55	10 Years	$64,000

But this $65,000 actually *beats* the $65,000 from either your pre-tax account or your brokerage account, because this $65,000 distribution is tax-free, which equates to a pre-tax distribution of $86,667 at a 25 percent tax rate. If you only had to pay tax on dividends and interest at 10 percent, for example, it would equal approximately a $72,222 distribution from a brokerage account. Contributing less over time, receiving more, and receiving it tax-free is a winning proposition. It gives hope for those who have a large personal retirement savings gap to make up for.

Tax Diversification and RMD Analysis

Many financial advisors are excellent at discussing diversification, asset diversification that is, within the three corners of the market. But have they ever discussed *tax diversification* with you? Have they analyzed the tax consequences of the income that will be produced from the assets you will have in retirement? I suspect most of you are saying no.

But remember what is so special about your retirement years: this is the one opportunity that you have in your life to decide your tax bracket.

Because this is so crucial, especially in a 2017 America and beyond, a large part of our practice is analyzing the tax consequences of the assets a client currently has going into retirement. We prepare a tax projection that spans their full retirement years.

We detail for them a RMD (Required Minimum Distribution) analysis, which shows what they will pay in taxes during their retirement years should they maintain the status-quo and keep their wealth pre-tax within their 401(k), IRA, TSP, or SEP. This analysis is compiled using current tax rates and does not account for a potential rise in taxes. This is in comparison to what they could pay if they decided to take control over their future by settling their account with the government and pay the tax over the next five years. We reposition their after-tax balance over this five-year period into a mix of a Roth and a properly structured life policy.

The tax savings are almost unbelievable.

Even people that have already built some wealth inside an IRA or a 401(k) will see tax advantages by moving their money into a properly structured life policy. By "controlling the burn" and moving the money in a controlled, strategic way, we can mitigate future tax consequences that could prevent you from achieving your strategic wealth goals.

By analyzing RMD projections over the lifetime of an IRA, my practice shows our clients just how much they'll save by switching to a tax-free vehicle that participates in and leverages market growth without the risk of market losses (the Roth balance remains subject to market losses).

For example, here is the analysis of a 52-year-old who currently has $500,000 saved within his 401(k). We run the RMD projections, beginning at the required age of 70 1/2 years old through age 90 (projected death), and we use a 4 percent growth rate on the account per year, net of all fees.

Potential Tax Impact

Base Case
Current Pre-Tax Qualified Account $500,000

The values below show two scenarios:

(1) The potential total taxes paid if you live to age 90, assuming you continue to keep your qualified account, take RMDs when required, and move those monies into a taxable account

(2) The total taxes paid if you live to age 90, assuming you roll over your qualified account to a Roth account today

Keep Qualified Account		Convert to Roth	
Total taxes paid on RMDs at time of withdrawals	$263,109	Taxes paid on conversion	$125,000
Taxes paid on reinvested RMDs	$107,890	Taxes paid on Roth account growth	$0
Taxes paid on remaining account value at death	$170,774	Taxes paid on remaining Roth account value at death:	$0
TOTAL TAXES PAID: **$541,773**			**$125,000**

RMD Calculation at 4%

IRA RMD Age	RMD Dist. Period	RMD	IRA CV @ 4% Assumed Int. Rate Less RMD	After Tax RMD	Acc at After-Tax Rate of 3%
53	0	$0.00	$520,000.00	$0.00	$0.00
54	0	$0.00	$540,800.00	$0.00	$0.00
55	0	$0.00	$562,432.00	$0.00	$0.00
56	0	$0.00	$584,929.28	$0.00	$0.00
57	0	$0.00	$608,326.45	$0.00	$0.00
58	0	$0.00	$632,659.51	$0.00	$0.00
59	0	$0.00	$657,965.89	$0.00	$0.00
60	0	$0.00	$684,284.53	$0.00	$0.00
61	0	$0.00	$711,655.91	$0.00	$0.00
62	0	$0.00	$740,122.14	$0.00	$0.00
63	0	$0.00	$769,727.03	$0.00	$0.00
64	0	$0.00	$800,516.11	$0.00	$0.00
65	0	$0.00	$832,536.75	$0.00	$0.00
66	0	$0.00	$865,838.22	$0.00	$0.00
67	0	$0.00	$900,471.75	$0.00	$0.00
68	0	$0.00	$936,490.62	$0.00	$0.00
69	0	$0.00	$973,950.25	$0.00	$0.00
70	27.40	$35,545.63	$977,362.63	$26,659.22	$26,659.22
71	26.50	$36,881.61	$979,575.52	$27,661.21	$55,120.21
72	25.60	$38,264.67	$980,493.87	$28,698.50	$85,472.32
73	24.70	$39,696.11	$980,017.52	$29,772.08	$117,808.57
74	23.80	$41,177.21	$978,041.01	$30,882.91	$152,225.74
75	22.90	$42,709.21	$974,453.44	$32,031.91	$188,824.42
76	22.00	$44,293.34	$969,138.24	$33,220.00	$227,709.15
77	21.20	$45,714.07	$962,189.70	$34,285.55	$268,825.97
78	20.30	$47,398.51	$953,278.77	$35,548.88	$312,439.63
79	19.50	$48,886.09	$942,523.84	$36,664.57	$358,477.39
80	18.70	$50,402.34	$929,822.45	$37,801.75	$407,033.46
81	17.90	$51,945.39	$915,069.96	$38,959.04	$458,203.50
82	17.10	$53,512.86	$898,159.90	$40,134.65	$512,084.26
83	16.30	$55,101.83	$878,984.46	$41,326.37	$568,773.16
84	15.50	$56,708.67	$857,435.17	$42,531.50	$628,367.85
85	14.80	$57,934.81	$833,797.77	$43,451.11	$690,670.00
86	14.10	$59,134.59	$808,015.09	$44,350.94	$755,741.04
87	13.40	$60,299.63	$780,036.00	$45,224.72	$823,637.69
88	12.70	$61,420.16	$749,817.34	$46,065.12	$894,412.25
89	12.00	$62,484.78	$717,325.26	$46,863.58	$968,108.20
90	11.40	$62,923.27	$683,095.00	$47,192.45	$1,044,343.90
91	10.80	$63,294.54	$647,169.26	$47,437.15	$1,123,111.37
92	10.20	$63,447.97	$609,608.06	$47,585.98	$1,204,390.69
93	9.60	$63,500.84	$570,491.54	$47,625.63	$1,288,148.04
94	9.10	$62,691.38	$530,619.82	$47,018.53	$1,373,811.01
95	8.60	$61,699.98	$490,144.63	$46,274.99	$1,461,300.33
96	8.10	$60,511.68	$449,238.74	$45,383.76	$1,550,523.10
97	7.60	$59,110.36	$408,097.93	$44,332.77	$1,641,371.56
98	7.10	$57,478.58	$366,043.27	$43,108.93	$1,733,721.64
99	6.70	$54,767.65	$326,853.35	$41,075.74	$1,826,809.03
100	6.30	$51,881.48	$288,046.00	$38,911.11	$1,920,524.41

In this example, you can see that we project total taxes of approximately $542,000 over this person's retirement (along with the tax his heirs will pay on the inherited balance) versus controlling the tax and paying it over the next five years. We use a life policy, alongside the Roth, to diminish our risk of loss due to market volatility which could prevent us from achieving our wealth goals.

Keep in mind, this analysis includes the tax you will pay on RMDs not spent but reinvested at a net 4 percent rate of return. However, many people *do* spend all their RMDs for their living expenses. So, we simply remove this additional tax and compare the figures without that additional amount. When we do this, we see that instead of saving $416,773 in taxes, we save $308,883.

In other words, based on *tax rates in 2017* (this is without considering *any* future tax increases), we still save hundreds of thousands of dollars. And over the next 20 years, these figures will be *grossly understated* as taxes must go up — it is a mathematical certainty.

And finally, here is an example RMD analysis for a 63-year-old who has accumulated $1 million in their IRA, with just a few years left before retirement. They would save $482,000 and, if they spent all their RMDs, would save $336,000.

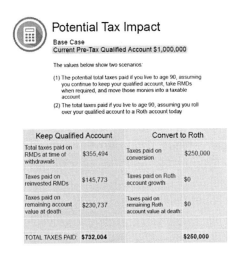

Potential Tax Impact

Base Case
Current Pre-Tax Qualified Account $1,000,000

The values below show two scenarios:

(1) The potential total taxes paid if you live to age 90, assuming you continue to keep your qualified account, take RMDs when required, and move those monies into a taxable account

(2) The total taxes paid if you live to age 90, assuming you roll over your qualified account to a Roth account today

Keep Qualified Account		Convert to Roth	
Total taxes paid on RMDs at time of withdrawals	$355,494	Taxes paid on conversion	$250,000
Taxes paid on reinvested RMDs	$145,773	Taxes paid on Roth account growth	$0
Taxes paid on remaining account value at death	$230,737	Taxes paid on remaining Roth account value at death:	$0
TOTAL TAXES PAID: $732,004		$250,000	

RMD Calculation at 4%

IRA RMD Age	RMD Dist. Period	RMD	IRA CV @ 4% Assumed Int. Rate Less RMD	After Tax RMD	Acc at After-Tax Rate of 3%
63	0	$0.00	$1,040,000.00	$0.00	$0.00
64	0	$0.00	$1,081,600.00	$0.00	$0.00
65	0	$0.00	$1,124,864.00	$0.00	$0.00
66	0	$0.00	$1,169,858.56	$0.00	$0.00
67	0	$0.00	$1,216,652.90	$0.00	$0.00
68	0	$0.00	$1,265,319.02	$0.00	$0.00
69	0	$0.00	$1,315,931.78	$0.00	$0.00
70	27.40	$48,026.71	$1,320,542.34	$36,020.03	$36,020.03
71	26.50	$49,831.79	$1,323,532.24	$37,373.84	$74,474.47
72	25.60	$51,700.45	$1,324,773.06	$38,775.36	$115,484.06
73	24.70	$53,634.54	$1,324,129.44	$40,225.90	$159,174.48
74	23.80	$55,635.69	$1,321,456.92	$41,726.77	$205,676.48
75	22.90	$57,705.63	$1,316,611.65	$43,279.22	$255,125.99
76	22.00	$59,845.98	$1,309,430.14	$44,884.49	$307,664.26
77	21.20	$61,765.57	$1,300,041.77	$46,324.18	$363,218.37
78	20.30	$64,041.47	$1,288,001.97	$48,031.10	$422,146.02
79	19.50	$66,051.38	$1,273,470.67	$49,538.54	$484,345.94
80	18.70	$68,100.04	$1,256,309.46	$51,075.03	$549,954.44
81	17.90	$70,184.69	$1,236,376.95	$52,638.67	$619,091.74
82	17.10	$72,302.75	$1,213,529.27	$54,227.06	$691,891.55
83	16.30	$74,449.65	$1,187,620.80	$55,837.24	$768,485.54
84	15.50	$76,620.70	$1,158,504.93	$57,465.52	$849,005.63
85	14.80	$78,277.36	$1,126,567.76	$58,708.02	$933,183.82
86	14.10	$79,898.42	$1,091,732.06	$59,923.82	$1,021,103.15
87	13.40	$81,472.54	$1,053,928.80	$61,104.40	$1,112,840.54
88	12.70	$82,986.52	$1,013,099.43	$62,239.89	$1,208,465.75
89	12.00	$84,424.95	$969,198.46	$63,318.71	$1,308,638.43
90	11.40	$85,017.41	$922,948.98	$63,763.06	$1,411,042.64
91	10.80	$85,458.24	$874,408.70	$64,093.68	$1,517,467.60
92	10.20	$85,726.34	$823,658.71	$64,294.75	$1,627,226.38
93	9.60	$85,797.78	$770,807.28	$64,348.33	$1,740,453.30
94	9.10	$84,704.10	$716,935.47	$63,528.08	$1,856,194.98
95	8.60	$83,364.59	$662,248.30	$62,523.44	$1,974,404.27
96	8.10	$81,759.05	$606,979.18	$61,319.29	$2,094,955.69
97	7.60	$79,865.68	$551,392.67	$59,899.26	$2,217,703.62
98	7.10	$77,660.94	$495,787.44	$58,245.71	$2,342,480.44
99	6.70	$73,998.12	$441,620.81	$55,498.59	$2,468,253.44
100	6.30	$70,095.54	$389,187.11	$52,573.90	$2,594,874.94

Again, these savings are *understated* because they do not incorporate rising tax rates over the next 10 years and beyond. These savings are based off of 2017 tax rates only.

As of this writing, the Senate is currently debating President Trump's 2017 tax reform proposal. What is frightening to me is the proposed Hatch Amendment, put forward by Republican senator Orrin Hatch, in which he aims to eliminate the ability to convert IRA and 401(k) money into a tax free Roth! Understand that you can pay the tax due on your pre-tax account at any time, but that is not the problem. What Hatch is proposing to eliminate is the ability to take the after-tax funds, once you have paid the tax, and move them into the Roth vehicle because Roth funds, including all of their growth, are never to be taxed again. So here, we can clearly see the government signaling that they cannot afford to lose these future tax revenues. Whether this reform gets through or not, the urgency of making these conversions while they remain possible is all the greater.

Many of my clients have already taken advantage of controlling their taxes by making the switch. They decided to settle their account, their tab with the government now, while tax rates are still at historical lows, so that their wealth can grow the rest of their life uncapped and untaxed. Understanding and seeing your RMDs in black and white is necessary for making good decisions about your wealth in retirement.

IUL - A Caveat or Two

As tax-advantaged as they are, there is a caveat to the IUL.

Some policies will boast a minimum guarantee even if the market experiences a downturn. For example, if the market experiences multiple year losses three years in a row, you would still see a 1 to 2 percent return.

But market losses three years in a row are an extremely rare occurrence.

Three years of consecutive losses have only happened three times since 1929. The first time was during the Great Depression, from 1929-1932. The second came during World War II, from 1939-1941. The third occurred when the dot-com bubble burst from 2000-2002.

In addition, even if you *do* experience a three or more year market downturn, those guaranteed returns are typically awarded at the *end* of the policy. Meaning they aren't subject to compound interest.

Some advisors may list this as a benefit, but in my experience, it's negligible. A 1 to 2 percent guaranteed return rate isn't something you should count on.

Other advisors, even some well-known national financial speakers, will say to 'keep insurance insurance and investments investments' because they say the costs of the insurance policy are high. But what they do not tell you is that term insurance policies — insurance policies that build no cash value and are solely designed to pay a death benefit — are so cheap and affordable because the insurance company expects a very low probability of actually paying out a benefit while you are young and well before your projected mortality age. In fact, only about 6 percent of term policies actually ever pay out the death benefit. And once the term policy expires, the cost to keep that same level of coverage in your later years, such as 60 and beyond, is so expensive that most people find it cost prohibitive and simply choose not to reinsure themselves. So just when you are getting near the age range of mortality to actually want the insurance benefit, what was very, very cheap now costs an arm and a leg.

This is not how a permanent policy works. Obviously, we are paying more in premiums than cheap term insurance, but that is because we are overfunding the policy to build cash value. And we are not throwing our money down the drain since we know that a death benefit will be paid when we pass, as the policy does not expire like a term policy does. Additionally, the cost differences between cheap term policies and permanent policies reflect the fact that permanent policies come with numerous living benefits that are effective immediately once the policy is in force. For example, all of the policies that we use allow your death benefit to be substantially advanced during life, tax-free, to pay for long-term care costs should you need such assistance.

To sum this up, there are many additional benefits that come with permanent life policies that simply do not exist by combining a cheap term policy with a market-based account. The value of these benefits, along with the assurance that you will have insurance coverage for life, makes for a superior option to wasting your money on a term policy that has literally a less than 10 percent probability of ever paying you back a penny and then becomes either too expensive to continue when you are older or you have become uninsurable along the way, which means that we couldn't secure coverage no matter the cost. To simply state that permanent life is more expensive than cheap term really misses the boat. The cost differential is more than justified by the benefits provided and worth it as long as the projected cash flow from our permanent policy in retirement satisfies our needs.

An IUL is one of the best ways to grow wealth through the market quickly and safely. And if you are still working and years from retirement, an IUL is an excellent alternative, or addition, after getting the match from your employer, for the funds you would have otherwise placed into a 401(k).

Whole Life

Although IULs are vehicles that provide strong, safe growth opportunities, we know that there will be years when the market will go down, causing our growth to remain flat. That growth will eventually pick up from the upside of market losses, but ultimately, IULs cannot guarantee a return rate year after year.

When we look to maximize growth as a *legacy*, we prefer to latch onto the compound yield curve in an uninterrupted way. Uninterrupted growth leaves us with only one option: the stalwart of life insurance, Whole Life.

Whole Life has been around longer than the Gerber baby because it was built to provide tax-advantaged positive returns *through all market cycles* for your entire life; thus the name "Whole Life".

Annual Gifting Strategy

Whole Life should deliver annual growth year after year of anywhere between 4 percent and 7 percent, on average.

I know that rate of return does not sound very exciting, but we have to remember that is uninterrupted growth year-over-year and is an after-tax number. So, that is the pre-tax equivalent of between 5.71 percent and 10 percent, at a 30 percent tax rate. For building lasting legacy wealth, these returns are more than sufficient.

At the very beginning of this book, I mentioned a client of mine that utilized a strategy to grow $1.26 million into a forecasted $45 million. We used multiple whole life policies with his family to build his legacy.

Let's re-examine that example to refresh our memories.

My client was a real estate developer who had done very well for himself. He already had a trust funded for his children and grandchildren, but still had additional resources to distribute. We showed him how to distribute those resources in the best way possible.

The annual gift limit that you can give to any single individual without filing a gift tax return is $14,000 in 2017.

My client could afford to give his nine grandchildren a gift of $14,000 per year, so we showed him what would happen if he gifted that each year, for 10 years, into a whole life policy for each grandchild, instead of using any other vehicle. For a total transfer of $1.26 million over 10 years, those nine separate accounts will grow into a forecasted $45 million by the time his grandchildren are at retirement age.

And remember, because that money has been growing within a life insurance policy, it will all be tax-free* when distributed, based on the current tax code, as it has been for over 100 years.

Because the grandchildren are minors, they cannot own the policies. Typically, we assign ownership to the parents and transfer the policies to each grandchild once they are financially responsible.

(As a side note, I personally would not recommend informing the child of the policy's existence any earlier than age 40. Time and time again, I've seen children's level of financial responsibility altered simply because they know they are inheriting millions of dollars. But of course, each child is different. Decisions should be made based on the respective character of each child.)

But this type of forecasted growth is contingent upon 10 years of uninterrupted deposits. We need to make sure the payments can be completed whether the financier is alive or dead.

In the event my client dies prematurely, we created a trust to safeguard the funding of the policies. The trust has enough cash in it to cover the balance of funding the policies, ensuring they are fully funded and never lapse.

Like I said, 4 percent to 7 percent might not seem like a super exciting amount, but it is more than sufficient because it compounds year after year, without fail, making these policies very attractive indeed.

Legacy Transfers

Whole Life is also a wonderful vehicle for legacy transfers. It's a tax-advantaged way to transfer wealth downwards.

And while it's more conservative, one of the benefits of Whole Life, as opposed to an IUL, is that it gives the policy holder an uninterrupted compound interest yield curve; the policy holder is always earning interest, year after year. (Remember, with an IUL, when the market goes down, occasionally the policy holder will see zero growth years, meaning interrupted growth.)

If you have already built wealth and you are looking to reposition it in a tax-advantaged way, Whole Life could be a better option for you. There could be another recession. There could be a period of zero market gains. Whole Life ensures your wealth is *always* growing, despite the volatility of the market.

These policies have been around for hundreds of years and are highly rated. It is likely these accounts will perform as projected, making them a confident, legacy building choice.

An IUL, in comparison, grows based on market performance. We can attempt to forecast growth based on index performance history, but we don't really know what will happen in the next 50 years.

Whole Life is going to give you growth, every single year, guaranteed. You might only get 4 percent growth, but over time, and with the help of compound interest, you will create substantial wealth.

How Much is This Going to Cost Me?

Another advantage to Whole Life is its price.

When policies are built, insurance companies basically average out the cost of your insurance as if you were going to live to the ripe old age of 121. Therefore, when you buy the policy, the costs are *guaranteed*. Unlike an IUL, the costs will not go up over time.

In the early years, a Whole Life policy will seem more expensive than an IUL. But because a Whole Life policy's fees are fixed, over time it will cost less than an IUL. With an IUL, you pay very little upfront, but as you get older, your premiums go up.

However, one of the problems associated with Whole Life is that expenses are not broken down within the policy. It's impossible to know exactly how your expenses are allocated. IUL is a little more transparent in this area.

A Bird in the Hand

Whole Life is an incredible wealth building tool. It offers tax-advantaged growth, uninterrupted compound interest, and fixed fees.

We've already talked about my client's incredible ability to turn $1.26 million into $45 million, but let's examine a few gifting strategies for someone who might be interested in the best ways to transfer wealth to grandchildren, as an example.

Take a look at the chart below that analyzes total growth from $14,000 in annual gift contributions for 10 years for a 1-year-old, a 10-year-old, and a 20-year-old.

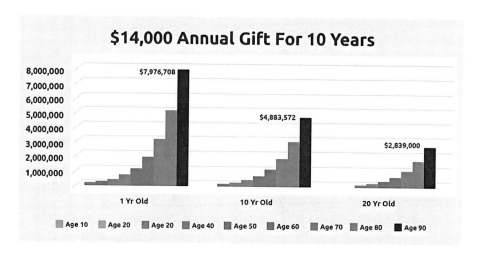

As you can see, for the full annual gift of $14,000, for just 10 years (a total gift of $140,000) we see that the 1-year-old's account grows to $8 million and the 10-year-old's grows to over $4.5 million.

It isn't too late to start something like this even if your child or grandchild is already 20. Even that account grows to over $2.8 million.

And again, these dollars are tax-free*.

Now, what do you think would happen if you simply gifted your child or grandchild the $140,000 outright? Do you think the money will be managed in a way that allows it to grow into millions of dollars, tax-free*?

It's very, very unlikely. As the saying goes, a bird in the hand...

A Gift that Could Not be Better Served

Whenever I think of legacy building and gift giving, I always picture a very specific scene.

The image that comes to mind features a young child sitting on the floor amongst her toys with a big, delighted smile on her face.

Surrounding the little girl are various names we call our grandparents. "Grammy, Me-maw, Nana, Nannie, Pop, Poppa, Gramps."

At the very bottom of the image the caption says:

> "Whatever they call you, make sure they remember you
> for the rest of their life."

By purchasing a Whole Life policy for grandchildren, not only are you passing down your legacy, you are providing them with the money needed to fund the various stages of their lives, not just for college, but for the rest of their lives.

As an example, let's go back to our 1-year-old, 10-year-old, and 20 year-old to whom we gifted $14,000 per year for 10 years. Let's see what using these funds solely for retirement would do for them.

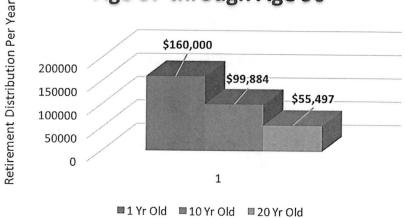

Annual Distributions Age 67 through Age 90

$160,000

$99,884

$55,497

Retirement Distribution Per Year

200000
150000
100000
50000
0

1

■ 1 Yr Old　■ 10 Yr Old　■ 20 Yr Old

**The amounts will vary with policy design and companies

Here, we project that the 1-year-old will enjoy a tax-free* distribution of $160,000 per year in retirement from ages 67 through age 90 and, during those same years, the 10-year-old will enjoy about $100,000 per year. Even the 20-year-old will enjoy about $55,000 per year tax-free* during their retirement years.

If $14,000 sounds like a lot of money to contribute, you're not alone.

Some of our clients have multiple grandchildren and cannot afford the $14,000 contribution for each or simply don't want to spend that much.

Even $2,500 a year for a 10 year period equating to a total gift of $25,000 per grandchild yields a decent return. For a 1-year-old, the $25,000 turns into $530,000, for a 10-year-old, it turns into $322,000 and for a 20-year-old, it turns into $192,000.

A gift that could not be better served.

Why Not You?

Let me be very clear.

As a tax attorney and wealth strategist, I have seen numerous, sophisticated financial transactions, including estate and trust planning, to reduce and control estate taxes. I've seen partnership transactions, corporate buy-outs, and liquidity at death utilizing buy-sell agreements that were funded by life policies. I have seen complicated corporate asset purchases of small businesses, newly appointed corporate executives, and commercial loans with personal guarantees. I have seen charitable LLCs with family trust buy-backs.

And what do all of these complicated, highly technical financial transactions have in common?

Only one thing: life insurance.

There is hardly a single high-level, high-finance transaction that does not contain life insurance as a component of the transaction.

This is how the wealthy keep their wealth and continue to see it grow. I've seen it time and time again. The richest of the rich utilize life insurance. And it has been that way for literally hundreds of years!

So, why not you? Why not *your* family?

Outside of real estate and a few certain stocks, life insurance, as an individual asset, is responsible for creating and injecting more intergenerational wealth than any other financial vehicle.

It should absolutely be a part of your wealth building picture.

But it cannot simply be any old life insurance policy. There are hundreds of carriers and thousands of policy designs. You need to work with an expert who is experienced and knows how to design the policy to maximize wealth.

Do not just go to the average insurance carrier and ask for a life policy. It likely will be quite a disappointment.

Work with someone who is a financial and tax expert. Make sure you are leveraging the best financial and tax tools available to you.

Typically, IUL and whole life policies provide tax-free income. However, if you have a modified endowment contract (MEC), the gain on the investment is taxable. MECs occur when you move your money too quickly. If you fund the policy over time, usually for at least five years, the gains are not taxable as long as you maintain the policy. If you surrender the policy, the gains will become taxable as well.

CHAPTER

12

Run Your
Own Race

Additional Strategies

We have certainly covered a lot, haven't we?

Together, we have established that when it comes to building wealth, most of America is simply on the wrong track and not in control of three major areas of creating wealth:

1. They are not allocating enough for their future self, creating an almost insurmountable, personal retirement savings gap;

2. They are subjecting most, if not all, of their wealth to the *New Normal* of extreme volatility of super highs followed by extraordinary lows that take years to recover from, losing real dollars forever from their wealth in the process; and

3. They have accumulated most, if not all, of their wealth in pre-tax mechanisms in which they have no control over how much they get to keep when they actually take distributions (since Uncle Sam is their silent partner inside these accounts).

These three deficiencies pack a powerful and debilitating punch to anyone's real ability to create lasting, sustainable wealth.

The result? Most Americans are not in control of their own financial destiny… Recall from our first chapter that only four out of 100 Americans actually achieve financial prosperity by age 65.

As if these glaring issues are not enough, America itself is headed into the perfect financial storm of our own creation. The retirement of our largest, organic born population, the Baby Boomers, colliding with the over $20 Trillion of National Debt – the result of 30+ years of sustained low federal tax policy during massive federal spending – combine to create an unprecedented financial tsunami headed our way.

With the majority of Americans not saving enough, deferring taxes, and relying on a volatile market to create their legacies, all during this unparalleled time in American history, we must stand up and *change direction*! Never before has a major financial course correction been more appropriate for the whole of our country.

We have walked through some strategies that we can incorporate with professional guidance and support that will very likely help us to reach our wealth building goals. Indexed Universal Life and Whole Life being a couple of those strategic options.

But of course, there is more to building wealth than life insurance. Life insurance, as the golden child of the U.S. tax code, is a perfect place to start, with both its living and legacy benefits inside of an unbeatable tax wrapper.

Beyond life insurance, we see that there are several additional complex financial concepts and options that should be leveraged as a part of an overall lasting and balanced financial strategy.

"Oh No, No, No"

Before we go into those options, I want to warn you: most financial advisors will not be open to many of the strategies in this book.

In addition to IUL and Whole Life policies, most advisors that exist solely within the market triangle view anything outside of stocks, bonds, and any variations thereof (mutual funds, index funds, ETFs, etc.), as atypical and not mainstream. And, if it does not exist within their market triangle, the option is automatically considered non-viable, and they will not be positive nor receptive to its use.

Outside the fact that of course they want you to keep your money in the market where they earn their fees on your balance, there is not much logic or reason presented as to why these options are not considered viable. A few might attempt to give you some feeble explanation and will rattle off something about being too expensive, but that can easily be proven to the contrary by breaking down the benefits of these strategies versus their costs and comparing those benefits and costs to a pure market-based portfolio and its associated money management fees.

Many financial advisors have been trained to look at wealth building in very specific ways, limiting their scope of knowledge to the dreaded triangle. Their expertise focuses solely on traditional wealth building categories of the market like stocks, bonds, and mutual funds.

Meaning, when you mention life insurance or *anything* that doesn't fit into their neat market triangle, you're probably going to hear, "Oh no, no, no."

The concepts from this book aren't solely mainstream wealth allocations. These concepts are innovative and simply don't register with most conventional advisors.

Expect push-back from traditional financial communities, but be prepared to defend your own strategic viewpoint as you've learned from this book. If your advisor was versed in the use of these strategies, then *they* would have brought their amazing benefits to your attention.

Distribution Strategies

In addition to the Roth, IULs, and Whole Life policies, there are a few other financial tools that are worth mentioning as they offer both growth and security. Annuities can be a fantastic supplement to use as a wealth building and preservation tool, and there are a thousand different flavors from which to choose.

Annuities are best utilized in two different ways: either to achieve market-based growth while eliminating the risk of loss, a growth annuity, or to replicate the pension system by creating a 'pension emulator' or a pension substitute, which we create using an income annuity. In fact, companies have utilized annuities themselves inside their pension funds in order to meet their pension obligations. [129]

Now, if you even mention annuities to your financial advisor, expect a big gasp and a disappointed head shake. Over the past 20 years, the product has earned a discouraging reputation. Let's uncover *why* a product that has the potential to be such a great tool has acquired such a reputation.

Insurance is all about the "law of large numbers." Anytime you're using an insurance based product, the company is basically calculating the following:

1. We are going to take a risk with you and add you to our large group of insureds;
2. We know that a few people within this large group will need benefits, but not everyone will need them;
3. As long as the whole does not need benefits, we can pay for the few that do and still make a profit.

That is how an insurance company can operate, provide benefits, and still make a profit through the "law of large numbers."

As a general overview of how annuities *used* to be, when people bought an annuity and died prematurely, the insurance company would keep the balance of their money. For example, if you bought a $200,000 annuity with a $10,000 annual payout and died after three years, the insurance company would keep the balance of $170,000.

But, on the opposite side, if someone contributed $200,000 to an annuity and lived to 103, they would have received $10,000 for 28 years, meaning that the insurance company more than paid them back. So, it all balanced out for the insurance company with enough profit for them to continue writing such business.

But it is hard to explain that to the loved ones of someone who died prematurely since they got the short end of the stick. It wasn't long before annuities got a bad reputation for short-changing people.

And rightfully so. Remember one of our goals is to "never lose money" so that, even in death, our heirs should reap the benefits of all the wealth that we have created.

Not What They Used to Be

But, those are the annuities of the past.

Annuities today make sense because we no longer lose our balance, even if we die young. Today, any unused funds are transferred down to your heirs. So, even when there is premature death, losing your money is no longer a risk.

Another concern, however, is their cost. But this is only a concern with variable annuities because a variable annuity is actively managed, charges high money management fees, and *can lose money*. For this reason, just as my firm does not use variable life policies, we likewise do not use variable annuities.

In contrast, the annuities we do use often have no fees at all and are not subject to market loss, because the growth is through options on an index just like an IUL.

Just like everything else in life, if you do not know the traps to avoid, any tool can be misused or inappropriately designed for your purposes, causing problems down the road. Leveraging an indexed growth or income annuity, with low to no fees, and no risk of loss that passes to heirs in the event of premature death, corrects the bad reputation that past annuities have garnered.

But too many will be easily persuaded to avoid their use because of the permanence of bad reputations. Do not allow anyone to so easily convince you not to use a tool that you actually may need to achieve your financial goals.

Pension Emulator / Pension Substitute

We use an **income annuity** to replicate the pensions of old, recreating our very own pension substitute.

When employers used to pay pensions, they retained all the risk of having to pay their retired employees for the rest of their lives, for as long as those employees remained alive. The risk of outliving your money is called **'longevity risk'** and this is one of the biggest advantages of a company pension.

Now that company pensions are a creature of the past for most Americans, we once again must deal with and resolve longevity risk on our own. So, by using an income annuity, we are again passing the risk of outliving our money onto someone else. In this case, that is an insurance company.

To simplify it, we basically invest the amount of money we are looking to use to supply our annual income for the rest of our lives. This pool of money will create a certain amount of annual income and, once we turn the distributions on, the insurance company will pay us that amount for as long as we live. If we live well into late life, we have mitigated the risk of running out of our money, since the insurance company will pay us until our deaths. And, if we pass early, our heirs will receive the balance of our investment, had we not been repaid it by the time we pass. This enables us to have a stress-free retirement income for life, disposing of the longevity risk completely!

Like everything else though, this is not an all or nothing strategy, and not everyone wants or even needs to fully reduce this risk. Perhaps we would employ this strategy partially, along with other strategies, so that the risk of living too long is not completely left on our shoulders.

The right balance of leveraging this tool is done on a case-by-case basis to fit your needs and requirements. However, if we do implement this guaranteed income plan, it acts as a 'safety cushion' which can free us up to be more aggressive towards pursuing growth in the balance of the portfolio. This guarantee of safe, lifetime income provides us a 'risk cushion' and empowers us to pursue more growth, more assertively because we have the certainty of a minimum income amount for the rest of our client's life.

Safe Growth in Retirement

Perhaps you have no risk of outliving your wealth as long as you protect what you have already built from the risk of loss. So, after building it through the accumulation phase of life, you simply want to protect it while continuing to grow it safely.

In other words, we want to have our cake and eat it, too.

We want growth, but not at the expense of losing some or all of our entire principal. This 'safe' growth is the appropriate growth goal for many that are in the distribution phase of their financial life cycle.

An excellent way to achieve such growth, outside of life insurance, is through a **growth annuity**. These annuities purchase options on various indexes and grow based on that index, but do not lose money, since the dollars are not directly invested in the market. Many of these vehicles come with low to no fees and have excellent performance track records.

Tax-Qualified Long-Term Care (LTC)

In addition to potentially eliminating longevity risk and growing wealth safely, many annuities today come with a long-term care (LTC) benefit for free.

If someone is not able to qualify for the more generous LTC benefits that come with most life policies, or if they do not want to use life policies for other reasons, then an annuity could be part of the answer. Rather than purchasing an expensive stand-alone long-term care policy, these annuities provide an additional option.

And annuities also work for those who are simply uninsurable.

Maybe you suffered from a heart attack in your 50s. Maybe you're a breast cancer survivor.

Unlike life insurance policies, annuities are a more inclusive vehicle for long-term care because they don't have any health requirements. Called tax-qualified long-term care, these annuities are like pension substitutes with long-term care, but without any of the health pre-qualifications. These annuities, in particular, provide the LTC benefit tax-free.

As one example, let's say that you have an income annuity that pays you an annual $20,000 distribution. Should the need arise for LTC, and you have this LTC protection within your annuity, the insurance company would *double* your income payment to $40,000 for up to five years as long as you still had the need for LTC. That additional $20,000 is not taxable, which is why it is called tax-qualified LTC.

Liquidity

In order for insurance companies to successfully write annuity business, remain profitable, and stay in business, there has to be some give and take. The annuities of today do this by simply restricting some access to your funds.

Many people misunderstand these restrictions and view this as a bad thing, and it could be if you had no access to your funds at all.

But this is not how an annuity works.

Most annuities provide the ability to access and cash-out anywhere from 7 percent to 10 percent of your entire balance every year for no cost or fee. If you need to access above the stated free percentage allowed in your contract, you can get your money but you simply have to pay a fee. However, in my experience, I find that the fee is much less than the fees associated with a managed account.

Let me give you an example.

Let's say a client purchases a $500,000 no-fee, growth annuity that has averaged a 7 percent return over the last 12 years. There is no risk of loss of principal and the client can access 7 percent of their principal balance every year for free. If they need to access more than 7 percent, they will pay a 10 percent fee on the amount that they withdraw above the 7 percent free limit.

Let's say the client needs to pull out $50,000, or 10 percent of their total balance. With the 7 percent free withdrawal per year, they are able to withdraw $35,000 for no fees or costs. But, since they need $15,000 above this amount, they will pay 10 percent of that $15,000, or a fee of $1,500 to the insurance company.

At first, this $1,500 fee might seem hefty, but it is actually less than the 1 percent management fee of $5,000 *per year* that this client would pay in a managed account on that same $500,000, *and* that managed account would be subject to the risk of loss in the market.

Thus, for a client that wants safe, solid growth with no fees, and wants to make this money last for at least 10 years, this financial option makes a lot of sense. The fees, even to withdraw 10 percent per year, every year, will be much less than the most common alternative of a managed money account charging an annual 1 percent management fee.

In other words, it is the best option for the client who wants safe growth, even with the reduced liquidity available. Remember, you can *always* get all of your money. It will just cost you a fee. For those that manage their access to their principal well and do not burn through their account, this account easily makes sense. And think about it: if this money is supposed to last you for the rest of your life, are you really going to access and spend it all within 10 years? Wouldn't you run out of money if you spent it that quickly anyway? For some clients, having this access restriction has proven to be quite beneficial.

Summing It Up

Regardless of what you may think or what you have been led to believe, annuities are a viable wealth building option and there may be a place for them within your wealth building strategy. Do not allow anyone to talk you out of looking at it as a viable option because "so and so" said it was bad for his friend's grandmother.

The annuities of today are not the annuities of yesterday. They aren't the annuities our grandparents or even our parents warned us about. My practice does not use, nor do we recommend the use, of the type of annuities that are ill-reputed because of their expensive fees and costs or because they have expensive rider charges.

The annuities of today can provide us with guaranteed income that we cannot outlive, and we use these to emulate the pensions of old that we are no longer able to get from our employer.

If you manage your wealth solely in the market, it is very probable that you will run out of money in retirement due to both market volatility and sequence of return risk. Monte Carlo analysis can show you this. For that reason, most people that stay 100 percent in the market seem to do so because they need aggressive growth to make up for their savings shortage. But for those who planned well and have no savings shortage, you have the luxury of not having to expose your entire portfolio to the risk of market losses at all times. If you have this luxury, why wouldn't you use it?

If you transfer money to an income annuity, a tool that contractually guarantees income for the rest of your life, you have eliminated your longevity risk and effectively eliminated the risk of outliving your money.

If you are not worried about running out of money, but you still need to protect what you have already built from loss when the market goes south, then a growth annuity might be for you. Of course, the right choice requires a professional consultation where your needs and wants are analyzed by an expert with knowledge of your personal financial situation.

Real Estate – A Wealth Builder

Pre-Tax Friendly

As we have discussed at length in Chapter Seven, future taxes are probably the single biggest threat to the security of your wealth.

However, some clients still prefer to maintain a portion of their wealth in pre-tax vehicles instead of converting it to a tax-free bucket over a five to 10 year period. For those that have funds built in a pre-tax account, there is still an exciting option which provides a long-term growth strategy.

If this is what you are looking for, real estate may be the answer.

Throughout America's history, real estate has been one of the best long-term wealth building strategies in existence. When you're looking at dollar for dollar appreciation over the history of our country, real estate has created more titans of industry than anything else.

But when it comes to wealth building and retirement, how do we leverage the power of real estate?

We purchase it through a wealth building tool.

Self-Directed IRAs and The '2 For 1' Asset Strategy

The self-directed IRA has existed since 1978.[130] Acquiring real estate is an excellent strategy for long term growth, and doing so within a self-directed IRA, when a client wants to retain the pre-tax nature of some of their funds, is an excellent choice.

I wouldn't be surprised if you've never heard of it, though. Many people are unaware that a self-directed IRA even exists.

This tool allows you to own many different asset classes, within your IRA (individual retirement account), at the same time. In addition to stocks and bonds, you can purchase leveraged real estate within your self-directed IRA.

My practice likes to take this process a step further: we combine leveraged residential real estate inside a pre-tax self-directed IRA with the tax benefits of life insurance. We particularly like to cultivate this strategy because we can create two assets with one dollar — our '2 For 1 Asset' strategy.

The base asset containing real estate grows in three ways:

1. The underlying real estate appreciates over time
2. The leverage is brought down over time through a tenant's rental payments (mortgage draw-down)
3. It generates net-positive cash flow, after expenses but before taxes, averaging approximately 8 percent to 10 percent per year (some properties generate more than 10 percent income)

We want the account to continue to grow in every aspect, but if we take the net rental income of 8 percent to 10 percent annually, we can use that cash flow, after tax, to fund a life policy, creating two assets from one.

With clients that already have a pre-tax account like a 401(k), IRA, 403(b), SIMPLE, SEP, or a TSP, we are able to do a simple rollover into the self-directed IRA. Once we do that, the funds are then used to purchase leveraged residential real estate. The net proceeds annually after taxes are used to fund an after-tax life policy.

Essentially, we have just converted pre-tax annual cash flow into a tax-free asset class.

The Power of Leverage

Buying leveraged real estate within a self-directed IRA is a little complicated, so let me walk you through an example to help explain.

If we roll $300,000 into a self-directed IRA using a third-party, the "custodian," we can actually buy approximately $600,000 worth of real estate because we can use a mortgage to buy real-estate inside one of a self-directed IRA. This is called leverage.

And partially because of this leverage, we can see real, substantial growth.

Over a 10 year period, the real estate asset continues to grow. Since the real estate is residential rental property, the client will see rental income. This income is partially used to pay down the leverage, the mortgage we used to buy the property to begin with.

When all these elements work together, a good estimate is that the $300,000 we initially invested will likely grow to net approximately $500,000 upon a sale within 10 years. (Remember, we actually purchased $600,000 of real estate that has appreciated over 10 years conservatively to $700,000+ and the mortgage has been paid down to $200,000).

Congruently, you are earning 8 to 10 percent cash flow on your $300,000 investment after expenses on that property. That's $24,000 of additional cash flow each year. We can then put the $24,000, after paying the tax on that income, into the tax-free vehicle of life insurance. This helps control the tax burn because we can siphon off cash flow on an annual basis, meaning the tax hit is expected to be rather small.

Over 10 years, we would have both a $240,000 fully funded life policy, and our original asset back having grown to $500,000, thus creating two assets from the $300,000 over a 10 year period.

Basically, by creating two assets from one, we now own both real estate and life insurance. One is tax free and the other remains pre-tax.

Had we simply kept the $300,000 in a pre-tax, market invested account and had it grown at an even 8 percent per year, in 10 years the account would be worth less than $650,000 and it would be 100% taxable. That *also* assumes no losses and a steady 8 percent rate of return every year for 10 straight years, which is impossible! Thanks to the *New Normal*, the CAGR (compound annual growth rate or annualized return) of the S&P 500 was 9.39 percent from 1990-2016, a period that included the longest bull market of our history, but only 4.47 percent from 2000-2016, a period that included the worst decade in S&P 500 history.[131]

Age Matters

But there is a caveat. We only suggest adding the outside life insurance component to a self-directed IRA cash flow when a client is 59 1/2 years or older so that we avoid the 10 percent tax penalty for withdrawing funds from a pre-tax account before that age.

This is a viable strategy outside of an IRA as well. If it is a concept you like, it can be done with after tax funds also, which would eliminate any age requirements.

Utilizing leveraged real estate in conjunction with a self-directed IRA or an after-tax account, like a brokerage account, is a really good way to create two assets with one dollar, creating both a tax-free account while growing the underlying real estate investment.

A lot of people are comfortable with real estate and don't like the ups and downs of the stock market. The use of a self-directed IRA, when you already have a bucket of pre-tax money that you want to maximize, is a great way to leverage real estate *inside* of retirement planning, while still allowing us to control the tax burn.

Real estate has its own risks though, just like investing in the market. An investor has to be aware of and comfortable with the risks associated with owning residential rental real estate in order for this to be a viable option. And if you are thinking that you do not know the first thing about buying residential rental real estate, getting it financed, or managing it, you're not alone. This is why we utilize a turn-key solution provided by a third-party company that has created an excellent niche in this unique space. They acquire the real estate, arrange the financing, manage the properties, and work with the custodian to ensure all the expenses are paid from your IRA account. They want the investment option to be as simple as buying a bond or investing in the market. That is probably not entirely possible since there are always unique issues to owning rental real estate, but they get pretty close for our clients.

Some Final Options

Many of you reading this book are either already retired or are approaching retirement. And some of you are looking for immediate income without delay.

There are options for you too.

My practice offers solutions that have historically paid between 6 and 8 percent of the principal amount, year after year, beginning immediately.

Most of the underlying investments have a real estate component, but your money is not actually buying or owning any real estate outright the way the self-directed IRA does. These funds have a proven track record and consistent performance and can be an excellent cash flow option. After a minimum period of time, usually at least two years, your original principal is returned. For those who seek a short-term option providing immediate and consistent income while preserving their underlying capital, this option can work.

Run Your Own Race

My practice, my life's work to date, and my passion have been dedicated to helping people grow wealth and build their legacy their way. For that to happen, a person must be an individual, able to stand on their own convictions, and able to '**run their own race**.'

This book does not speak solely to mainstream wealth building strategies. There are hundreds of those and I suspect that, if you had wanted to read about mainstream methods, you would have bought a more conventional book.

The solutions *we've* discussed are some of the best kept secrets of the financial world, solutions used by the wealthiest elite. You can go to a traditional advisor and you will get exactly what you would expect: conventional wisdom. Or you can get serious about not becoming a part of the 96 percent of America that fails to achieve financial prosperity in retirement and *decide to take the road less traveled*. Ask yourself what is so wonderful about convention if it results in 96 percent of everyone not achieving real success.

Convention has failed. It is just that simple. Truly beginning to create your legacy takes work and it takes doing things differently *intentionally*.

Controlling your financial destiny requires being in a position to control your own wealth and your own future.

At the end of the day, it isn't about where you start or where you are right now. All that matters is where you finish your race.

So, listen to the voice inside of you that is telling you there must be a better way. Do not be discouraged by the naysayers — the 96 out of 100 that will fail to achieve true financial success —and *run your own race!* Build your legacy and make it last throughout the generations.

Acknowledgments

Wow. I am so happy to be at this page and finishing such an important piece of work. Writing a book of this magnitude has been an incredibly challenging experience while running my practice and being a wife and mother. It is only the absolute and unwavering conviction I have for this specific message and disseminating it to as many as have ears to hear that such a sacrifice of time, energy, and resources have made it well worth it.

First, I would like to thank my husband and soul mate of over 15 years, Ron, who has demonstrated the character and patience of a saint. You have been my encouragement, my rock, and my world for nearly two decades, and without you, none of this would have been possible or worthwhile.

Thank you to my children for putting up with my supersized schedule and temporarily distracted frame of mind and to Nana for being the best grandparent and mother-in-law a girl could ever have wished for.

Thank you to Wid Bastian for your guidance and expert direction and to Brett Kitchen and Ethan Kap for helping me recognize the book I had within me. Thank you to Doug Brown, Jack Bussell, and Danielle Lieneman of Atlantic Publishing and to Lisa and Katie for your crafting and honing of my words into the most useful and consequential content.

Thank you to my Walser Wealth Team for your unwavering support and superior dedication to our mission of making a real difference in our clients' lives and for just making work a great place to be.

Thank you to you, the readers of Wealth Unbroken. My hopes are that it reveals a great deal regarding the state of America, where we have been and where we are headed and what you can do NOW to take back control over your own financial destiny by running your own race.

Finally, and most importantly, I am most grateful to my heavenly Father and my Lord and Savior, Jesus Christ, the author and finisher of my faith, without whom nothing of earthly importance has any meaning.

End Notes

1. "Titanic," Directed by James Cameron. Hollywood, CA: Twentieth Century Fox, Paramount Pictures, and Lightstorm Entertainment, 1997.

2. Dan Miner, "Priceline.com entrepreneur: Innovation is not an accident," *Buffalo Business First*, (August 19, 2014) **https://www.bizjournals.com/buffalo/news/2014/08/19/priceline-com-entrepreneur-innovation-is-not-an.html** (accessed July 22, 2017).

3. W. Michael Cox and Richard Alm, "Creative Destruction," *Library of Economics and Liberty*, **http://www.econlib.org/library/Enc/CreativeDestruction.html** (accessed July 22, 2017).

4. Mark Weinberger, "Why entrepreneurs are essential to the global economy." Financial Times. (June 6, 2016) **https://www.ft.com/content/c1d2736c-1cdc-11e6-a7bc-ee846770ec15** (accessed May 24, 2017).

5. "Imperialism and Colonialism, 1870-1914," *Western Civilizations*, W.W. Norton & Company, Inc., **http://www.wwnorton.com/college/history/western-civilization17/ch/22/outline.aspx** (accessed July 22, 2017).

6. James Rainey, "Oscars: LAPD Plans for 'Multiple Scenarios' With Three Tiers of Security," *Variety*, (February 24, 2017) **https://variety.**

com/2017/film/news/oscars-2017-security-police-rain-trump-forecast-1201995916/ (accessed May 29, 2017).

7. Michelle Goldberg, "What is a Woman?" *The New Yorker*, (August 4, 2014) **http://www.newyorker.com/magazine/2014/08/04/woman-2** (accessed May 29, 2017).

8. Nathaniel Parish Flannery, "Has Venezuela's Economic Crisis Reached A Breaking Point?" *Forbes*, (May 15, 2017) **http://www.forbes.com/sites/nathanielparishflannery/2017/05/15/has-venezuelas-economic-crisis-reached-a-breaking-point/#5472f72f2f79** (accessed May 29, 2017).

9. Emiliana Disilvestro, "Venezuela's Bizarre System of Exchange Rates," *Mises Institution*, (July 1, 2016) **https://mises.org/library/venezuelas-bizarre-system-exchange-rates** (accessed May 29, 2017).

10. Jim Wyss, "Venezuela has a bread shortage. The government has decided bakers are the problem," *The Miami Herald*, (March 16, 2017) **http://www.miamiherald.com/news/nation-world/world/americas/venezuela/article138964428.html** (accessed May 29, 2017).

11. "Venezuela crisis: What is behind the turmoil?" *BBC News*, (May 4, 2017) **http://www.bbc.com/news/world-latin-america-36319877** (accessed July 16, 2017).

12. "Goodreads Quotable Quotes: Abraham Lincoln," *Goodreads*, **https://www.goodreads.com/quotes/8140172-you-cannot-help-the-poor-by-destroying-the-rich-you** (accessed July 23, 2017).

13. "Free Market," *Dictionary.com*, **http://www.dictionary.com/browse/free-market** (accessed May 29, 2017).

14. Peter Ferrara "The Way The World – And Free-Market Economics – Works." *Forbes*, (December 22, 2011) **https://www.forbes.com/sites/peterferrara/2011/12/22/the-way-the-world-and-free-market-economics-works/#2c2af83862b4** (accessed May 29, 2017).

15. Lauren Thomas, "Universal basic income debate sharpens as observers grasp for solutions to inequality," *CNBC*, (March 25, 2017) **http://www.cnbc.com/2017/03/25/universal-basic-income-debate-sharpens.html** (accessed July 23, 2017).

16. Andrew Griffin, "Mark Zuckerberg Calls for Universal Basic Income Amid Rumors of Presidential Bid," *Independent*, (May 26, 2017) **https://www.independent.co.uk/life-style/gadgets-and-tech/news/mark-zuckerberg-universal-basic-income-harvard-commencement-speech-facebook-president-bid-a7757781.html** (accessed May 29, 2017).

17. "Band," *U2*, **http://www.u2.com/band** (accessed May 30, 2017).

18. Mark Hendrickson, "U2's Bono Courageously Embraces Capitalism," *Forbes*, (November 8, 2013) **https://www.forbes.com/sites/markhendrickson/2013/11/08/u2s-bono-courageously-embraces-capitalism/2/#655e60027f3f** (accessed May 30, 2017).

19. Fan Gang, "China Is a Private-Sector Economy," Bloomberg Businessweek, (August 21, 2055) **https://www.bloomberg.com/news/articles/2005-08-21/online-extra-china-is-a-private-sector-economy** (accessed July 23, 2017).

20. Lesley Stahl, "China's Real-Estate Bubble," *60 Minutes*, (August 3, 2014) **http://www.cbsnews.com/videos/nobodys-home-the-ghost-cities-of-china/** (accessed May 30, 2017).

21. "Surveying the Ghost Cities of China," *Priceonomics*, (November 19, 2015) **https://priceonomics.com/surveying-the-ghost-cities-of-china/** (accessed July 23, 2017).

22. "China turmoil pushes global stocks towards worst start to a year in at least 28 years," *thestar.com*, (January 7, 2016) **https://www.thestar.com/news/world/2016/01/07/stocks-worldwide-retreat-on-fears-china-slump-is-worsening.html** (accessed July 23, 2017).

23. Steve Inskeep and David Wessel, "What The Drop In Commodity Prices Means For The U.S. Economy," *NPR*, (January 19, 2016) **http://www.npr.org/2016/01/19/463551017/what-the-drop-in-commodity-prices-means-for-the-u-s-economy** (accessed July 23, 2017).

24. Adam Shell, "S&P 500 off to worst-ever start to year," *USA Today*, (January 6, 2016) **https://www.usatoday.com/story/money/markets/2016/01/06/china-stocks/78390650/** (accessed July 23, 2017).

25. Tyler Durden, "$1,001,000,000,000: China Just Flooded Its Economy With A Record Amount Of New Debt," *ZeroHedge*, (April 15, 2016) **http://**

www.zerohedge.com/news/2016-04-15/1001000000000-china-just-flooded-its-economy-record-amount-new-debt (accessed July 23, 2017).

26. "China Population," *Trading Economics,* https://tradingeconomics.com/china/population (accessed May 30, 2017).

27. "China's personal income rises 6.3 pct in 2016," *Global Economics,* (Jan 20, 2017) http://www.globaltimes.cn/content/1029839.shtml (accessed July 23, 2017).

28. "United States Population," *Trading Economics,* https://tradingeconomics.com/united-states/population (accessed May 30, 2017).

29. "Per capita disposable personal income in the United States in 2016, by state (in U.S. dollars)," *Statista,* (2017) https://www.statista.com/statistics/303534/us-per-capita-disposable-personal-income/ (accessed July 23, 2017).

30. Steve Inskeep and David Wessel (accessed July 23, 2017).

31. "Gold, Money, and the Gold Standard," *World Gold Council,* http://www.gold.org/history-and-facts/gold-money (Accessed June 5, 2017).

32. Smith, Adam, *An Inquiry into the Nature and Causes of the Wealth of Nations* (London: W. Strahan and T. Cadell, 1776).

33. Frank Holmes, "A history of the US gold standard" *Business Insider,* (December 10, 2015) http://www.businessinsider.com/history-of-us-gold-standard-2015-12 (accessed July 23, 2017).

34. Roosevelt, Franklin D., "34-Executive Order 6102-Requiring Gold Coin, Gold Bullion and Gold Certificates to Be Delivered to the Government," (April 5, 1933).

35. "FDR takes United States off gold standard," *History.com,* https://www.history.com/this-day-in-history/fdr-takes-united-states-off-gold-standard (accessed July 23, 2017).

36. The Gale Group, Inc., "Gold Standard," *Encyclopedia.com,* (2003) http://www.encyclopedia.com/social-sciences-and-law/economics-business-and-labor/money-banking-and-investment/gold-standard (accessed July 23, 2017).

37. Frank Holmes, "Top 10 Countries With The Largest Gold Reserves," *Forbes,* (May 26, 2016) https://www.forbes.com/sites/

greatspeculations/2016/05/26/top-10-countries-with-the-largest-gold-reserves/2/#1b7cfb9a22db (accessed July 23, 2017).

38. Louis G. Navellier, "Celebrating 40 Years of Gold Freedom (After 40+ Years of Gold Prohibition)," *Navellier Gold*, (August 20, 2014) **https://www.navelliergold.com/celebrating-40-years-of gold-freedom-after-40-years-of-gold-prohibition/** (accessed July 23, 2017).

39. David Kennedy, "The Great Depression and World War II, 1929-1945," *The Gilder Lehrman Institute of American History*, **https://www.gilderlehrman.org/history-by-era/essays/great-depression-and-world-war-ii-1929-1945** (accessed July 23, 2017).

40. "Abandonment of Gold Standard during Inter-War Period," *Middlebury College*, **https://mediawiki.middlebury.edu/wiki/IPE/Abandonment_of_Gold_Standard_during_Inter-War_Period** (accessed July 23, 2017).

41. "Nixon and the End of the Bretton Woods System, 1971-1973," *Office of the Historian*, **https://history.state.gov/milestones/1969-1976/nixon-shock** (accessed June 5, 2017).

42. Ayse Evrensel, "RESERVE CURRENCY SYSTEM ESTABLISHED AT THE BRETTON WOODS CONFERENCE," *dummies.com*, **http://www.dummies.com/education/finance/international-finance/reserve-currency-system-established-at-the-bretton-woods-conference/** (accessed July 23, 2017).

43. *Evrensel* (accessed July 23, 2017).

44. "Nixon Ends Convertibility of US Dollars to Gold and Announces Wage/Price Controls," *Federal Reserve History*, (August 1971) **https://www.federalreservehistory.org/essays/gold_convertibility_ends** (accessed June 5, 2017).

45. Kimberly Amadeo, "What Is the History of the Gold Standard? (June 2, 2017) *TheBalance.com*, **https://www.thebalance.com/what-is-the-history-of-the-gold-standard-3306136** (accessed July 23, 2017).

46. "Special Drawing Right SDR," *International Money Fund*, (April 21, 2017) **http://www.imf.org/en/About/Factsheets/Sheets/2016/08/01/14/51/Special-Drawing-Right-SDR** (accessed August 14, 2017).

47. Linette Lopez, "China's economy is at the mercy of a force completely beyond its control," *Business Insider,* (Jan 12, 2017) **http://www.businessinsider.com/how-a-strong-dollar-is-hurting-china-2017-1** (accessed August 14, 2017).

48. Phoenix Capital Research, "Could China Demand the US Dollar Lose Reserve Currency Status," *ZeroHedge.com,* (December 29, 2016) **http://www.zerohedge.com/news/2016-12-29/could-china-demand-us-dollar-lose-reserve-currency-status** (accessed August 14, 2017).

49. Joe McDonald and Buisness Writer, "China calls for new global currency," *ABC News,* **http://abcnews.go.com/Business/story?id=7168919&page=1** (accessed August 14, 2017).

50. "What is the deficit?" *USGovernmentSpending.com,* **http://www.usgovernmentspending.com/federal_deficit_chart.html** (accessed August 14, 2017).

51. Barbara A. Butrica, Howard M. Iams, Karen E. Smith, and Eric J. Toder, "The Disappearing Defined Benefit Pension and Its Potential Impact on the Retirement Incomes of Baby Boomers," *Social Security Bulletin*, Vol. 69, No. 3, (2009) **https://www.ssa.gov/policy/docs/ssb/v69n3/v69n3p1.html** (accessed July 3, 2017).

52. "A brief history of 401K," *Benna401k,* **http://401kbenna.com/401k-history.html** (accessed July 23, 2017).

53. "A Look at Private-Sector Retirement Plan Income After ERISA," *Investment Company Institute Research Perspective,* Vol. 16, No. 2, (November 2010) **https://www.ici.org/pdf/per16-02.pdf** (accessed July 3, 2017).

54. Butricia, Iams, Smith, and Toder (accessed July 3, 2017).

55. Steven Porter, "Why 'Father of the 401(k)' says he regrets pushing the retirement plan," *The Christian Science Monitor,* (Jan. 4, 2017) **https://www.csmonitor.com/Business/2017/0104/Why-Father-of-the-401-k-says-he-regrets-pushing-the-retirement-plan** (accessed July 23, 2017).

56. Stoyan Panayotov, "What's the difference between a 401(k) and a pension plan?" *Investopedia,* **http://www.investopedia.com/ask/**

answers/100314/whats-difference-between-401k-and-pension-plan.asp (accessed July 3, 2017).

57. Monique Morrissey, "Private-sector pension coverage fell by half over two decades," *Economic Policy Institute*, (January 11, 2013) **http://www.epi.org/blog/private-sector-pension-coverage-decline/** (accessed July 3, 2017).

58. Butricia, Iams, Smith, and Toder (accessed July 3, 2017).

59. Jason M. Breslow, "Teresa Ghilarducci: Why the 401(k) is a "Failed Experiment," *PBS Frontline*, (April 23, 2013) **http://www.pbs.org/wgbh/frontline/article/teresa-ghilarducci-why-the-401k-is-a-failed-experiment/** (accessed July 3, 2017).

60. "Compound Annual Growth Rate (Annualized Return)," *MoneyChimp.com*, **http://www.moneychimp.com/features/market_cagr.htm** (accessed August 14, 2017).

61. "Compound Annual Growth Rate (Annualized Return)," (accessed August 14, 2017).

62. Sean Hanlon, "Why The Average Investor's Investment Return Is So Low," *Forbes*, (April 24, 2014) **https://www.forbes.com/sites/advisor/2014/04/24/why-the-average-investors-investment-return-is-so-low/#9ca3af1111a3** (accessed July 3, 2014).

63. Tim Parker, "What's the Average 401(k) Balance by Age?" *Investopedia*, (June 7, 2017) **http://www.investopedia.com/articles/personal-finance/010616/whats-average-401k-balance-age.asp?lgl=rira-baseline** (accessed July 23, 2017).

64. David Dayen, "The Retirement Revolution that Failed" Why the 401(k) Isn't Working," *TheFiscalTimes*, (March 4, 2016) **http://www.thefiscaltimes.com/Columns/2016/03/04/Retirement-Revolution-Failed-Why-401k-Isn-t-Working** (accessed July 3, 2017).

65. Matthew Frankel, "The Average American's 401(k) Balance Has Never Been Higher -- But It's Still Not Enough" *The Fool,* (Feb 12, 2017) **https://www.fool.com/investing/2017/02/12/the-average-americans-401k-balance-has-never-been.aspx** (accessed July 23, 2017).

66. Dayen (accessed July 3, 2017).

67. Parker (accessed July 23, 2017).

68. Robert Preidt, "Most Mt. Everest Deaths Occur Near Summit During Descent," *ABC News*, (Dec 12, 2009) **http://abcnews.go.com/Health/ Healthday/story?id=6445450&page=1** (accessed June 7, 2017).

69. Jen Wieszner, "Happy Birthday, Bull Market! It May Be Your Last," *Fortune*, (Mar 9, 2017) **http://fortune.com/2017/03/09/stock-market-bull-market-longest/** (accessed July 25, 2017).

70. Wieszner (accessed July 25, 2017).

71. "The Great Recession," *Investopedia*, **http://www.investopedia.com/ terms/g/great-recession.asp** (Accessed June 7, 2017).

72. Robert Rich, "The Great Recession," *Federal Reserve Bank of New York*, (November 22, 2013) **https://www.federalreservehistory.org/essays/ great_recession_of_200709** (accessed July 25, 2017).

73. Benoît Cœuré, "The economic consequences of low interst rates," *International Center for Monetary and Banking Studies*, Geneva, Switzerland, (October 9, 2013) **https://www.ecb.europa.eu/press/key/date/2013/html/ sp131009.en.html** (accessed July 25, 2017).

74. Elena Holodny, "The 5,000-year history of interest rates shows just how historically low US rates are right now," *Business Insider*, (June 17, 2016) **http://www.businessinsider.com/chart-5000-years-of-interest-rates-history-2016-6** (accessed June 7, 2017).

75. Jonathan Soble, "Japan's Negative Interest Rates Explained," *The New York Times*, (September 20, 2016) **https://www.nytimes.com/2016/09/21/ business/international/japan-boj-negative-interest-rates.html** (accessed July 25, 2017).

76. "Germany becomes second G-7 nation to issue 1-=year bond with negative yield," *Reuters*, (July 13, 2016) **http://www.cnbc.com/2016/07/13/ germany-becomes-second-g7-nation-to-issue-10-year-bond-with-a-negative-yield.html** (accessed July 25, 2017).

77. "Germany becomes second G-7 nation to issue 10-year bond with negative yield," (accessed June 7, 2017).

78. Randall Smith, "Why the 4% Retirement Rule Is No Longer Safe," *Investopedia*, **http://www.investopedia.com/articles/personal-**

finance/120513/why-4-retirement-rule-no-longer-safe.asp (accessed June 7, 2017).

79. David Blanchette, CFA, CFP, Michael Fink, Ph. D, CFP, Wade D. Pfau, Ph. D, CFP, "Low Bond Yields and Safe Portfolio Withdrawal Rates," *Morningstar Investment Management*, (January, 21, 2013).

80. Dan Caplinger, "5 Money-Making Lessons from 2008's Market Crash," *AOL.com*, (September 15, 2013) **https://www.aol.com/article/finance/2013/09/15/money-making-investing-lessons-2008-market-crash/20720446/** (August 14, 2017).

81. Mark Hulbert, "25 Years to Bounce Back? Try 4½," *The New York Times*, (April 25, 2009) **http://www.nytimes.com/2009/04/26/your-money/stocks-and-bonds/26stra.html** (accessed August 14, 2017).

82. Tim Mullaney, "8 things you need to know about bear markets," *CNBC*, (Aug 24, 2015) **http://www.cnbc.com/2015/08/24/8-things-you-need-to-know-about-bear-markets.html** (accessed July 25, 2017).

83. Walter Mischel and Ebbe B. Ebbesen, "Attention in delay of gratification," *Journal of Personality and Social Psychology*, Vol 16(2) (October 1970) DOI: 10.1037/h0029815 (accessed June 25, 2017).

84. Mischel and Ebbesen (accessed June 25, 2017).

85. Walter Mischel, Yuichi Shoda, Monica L. Rodriguez, "Delay of gratification in children," *Science*, Vol. 244, Issue 4907, (May 26, 1989) DOI: 10.1126/science.2658056 (accessed June 25, 2017).

86. Tanya R. Schlam, PhD, Nicole L. Wilson, PhD, Yuichi Shoda, PhD, Walter Mischel, PhD, Ozlem Ayduk, PhD, "Preschoolers' Delay of Gratification Predicts their Body Mass 30 Years Later," *The Journal of Pediatrics*, Volume 162, Issue 1 (January 2013) DOI: **http://dx.doi.org/10.1016/j.jpeds.2012.06.049** (accessed June 25, 2017).

87. Walter Mischel, Ebbe B. Ebbesen, Raskoff Zeiss, Antoinette, "Cognitive and attentional mechanisms in delay of gratification," *Journal of Personality and Social Psychology*, Vol 21(2), (February 1972) DOI:10.1037/h0032198 (accessed June 25, 2017).

88. Yuichi Shoda, Walter Mischel, Philip K. Peake, "Predicting adolescent cognitive and self-regulatory competencies from preschool delay in

gratification: Identifying diagnostic conditions," *Developmental Psychology*, Vol 26(6) (November 1990) DOI:10.1037/0012-1649.26.6.978 (accessed June 25, 2017).

89. Monique Morrissey, "The State of American Retirement," *Economic Policy Institute*, (March 3, 2016) **http://www.epi.org/publication/retirement-in-america/** (accessed July 24. 2017).

90. Stephen Gandel, "Why It's Time to retire the 401(k)," *Time*, (October 9, 2009) **https://content.time.com/time/magazine/article/0,9171,1929233,00.html** (accessed July 24, 2017).

91. "How Do Benefits Compare to Earnings?" *National Academy of Social Insurance*, **https://www.nasi.org/learn/socialsecurity/benefits-compare-earnings** (accessed August 14, 2017).

92. Tyler Durden, "Poland Confiscates Half Of Private Pension Funds To "Cut" Sovereign Debt Load," *ZeroHedge*, (September 6, 2013) **http://www.zerohedge.com/news/2013-09-06/poland-confiscates-half-private-pension-funds-cut-sovereign-debt-load** (accessed July 24, 2017).

93. Marek Strzelecki, Maciej Onoszko, Marta Waldoch, "Polish Pension Revamp Targets $35 Billion of Private Funds," *Bloomberg*, (July 4, 2016) **https://www.bloomberg.com/news/articles/2016-07-04/poland-to-overhaul-its-35-billion-private-pension-fund-industry** (accessed June 25, 2017).

94. "Update 2-Poland announces big shakeup in pension systems," *Reuters*, (July 4, 2016) **http://www.reuters.com/article/poland-pensions-idUSL8N19Q134** (accessed July 24, 2017).

95. Historical Debt Outstanding – Annual 1950-1999" *TreasuryDirect*, **https://www.treasurydirect.gov/govt/reports/pd/histdebt/histdebt_histo4.htm** (accessed July 24, 2017).

96. Charles Kadlec, "Nixon's Colossal Monetary Error: The Verdict 40 Years Later," *Forbes*, (August 15, 2011) **https://www.forbes.com/sites/charleskadlec/2011/08/15/nixons-colossal-monetary-error-the-verdict-40-years-later/#57aa1f9b69f7** (accessed July 24, 2017).

97. "Life Expectancy for Social Security," *Social Security History*, **https://www. ssa.gov/history/lifeexpect.html** (accessed July 24. 2017).

98. *Board of Trustees of the Federal Old–Age and Survivors Insurance and Federal Disability Insurance Trust Funds, "The 2012 Annual Report of the Board of Trustees of the Federal Old–Age and Survivors Insurance and Federal Disability Insurance Trust Funds,"* Washington, D.C., (April 23, 2012) **https://www.ssa.gov/oact/TR/2012/tr2012.pdf** (accessed July 24, 2017).

99. "Baby Boomers Retire," *Pew Research Center*, (December 29, 2010) **http://www.pewresearch.org/fact-tank/2010/12/29/baby-boomers-retire/** (accessed July 24, 2017).

100. "David M. Walker," *Wikipedia*, **https://en.wikipedia.org/wiki/David_M._ Walker_(U.S._Comptroller_General)** (accessed July 24, 2017).

101. Congressional Budget Office, "Letter to Congressman Paul Ryan," *U.S. Congress*, (May 19. 2008), **https://www.cbo.gov/sites/default/files/110th-congress-2007-2008/reports/05-19-longtermbudget_letter-to-ryan.pdf** (accessed July 24, 2017).

102. "History of Federal Income Tax Rates: 1913-2017," *Bradford Tax Institute*, **https://bradfordtaxinstitute.com/Free_Resources/Federal-Income-Tax-Rates.aspx** (accessed July 24, 2017).

103. "Top Federal Income Tax Rates Since 1913," *CTJ.org*, (November, 2011) **http://www.ctj.org/pdf/regcg.pdf** (accessed July 24, 2017).

104. David Schepp, "How Auto-Escalation Can Help You Save More for Retirement," *U.S. News*, (January 27, 2016) **https://money.usnews.com/ investing/articles/2016-01-27/how-auto-escalation-can-help-you-save-more-for-retirement** (accessed July 24, 2017).

105. "Roth IRA Withdrawal Rules," *Charles Schwab*, **http://www.schwab.com/public/schwab/investing/retirement_and_ planning/understanding_iras/roth_ira/withdrawal_rules** (accessed July 24, 2017).

106. "409A Nonqualified Deferred Compensation Plans," *IRS*, **https://www.irs. gov/retirement-plans/409a-nonqualified-deferred-compensation-plans** (accessed July 2, 2017).

107. Cam Marston, "Great wealth transfer will be $30 trillion-yes, that's trillion with a T," *CNBC*, (July 22, 2014) **http://www.cnbc.com/2014/07/22/ great-wealth-transfer-will-be-30-trillionyes-thats-trillion-with-a-t.html** (accessed June 25, 2017).

108. Nick Thornton, "Total retirement assets near $25 trillion mark," *BenefitsPro*, (June 30, 2015) **http://www.benefitspro.com/2015/06/30/total- retirement-assets-near-25-trillion-mark** (accessed July 24, 2017).

109. "Asset Protecting Inherited IRAs," *Dean Jones LLP*, **http://deanjonesllp. com/Page/asset-protecting-inherited-iras** (accessed July 24, 2017).

110. "US. Debt Clock.org" **http://www.usdebtclock.org/** (accessed June 25, 2017).

111. Robert A. Ross, "Six biggest IRA Beneficiary Form Mistakes," *Steve Shaw Law*, **http://www.steveshawlaw.com/index.php/2012-06-12- 15-42-03/20-blog-articles/estate-planning/69-irs-statistics-show-us- that-90-of-ira-s-are-cashed-out-within-6-months-of-death** (accessed July 24, 2017).

112. Nari Rhee, PhD, "The Retirement Savings Crisis: Is It Worse Than We Think?" *National Institute on Retirement Security*, (June 2013) **http://www.nirsonline.org/storage/nirs/documents/Retirement%20 Savings%20Crisis/retirementsavingscrisis_final.pdf** (accessed June 26, 2017).

113. Bloomberg News, "Report predicts $400 trillion retirement savings gap by 2050," *Investment News*, (May 26, 2017) **http://www.investmentnews. com/article/20170526/FREE/170529938/report-predicts-400-trillion- retirement-savings-gap-by-2050** (accessed August 14, 2017).

114. Daniel Wesley, "A Lifetime of Debt: The financial Journey of the Average American," *CreditLoan.com*, (May 3, 2017) **https://www.creditloan.com/blog/a-lifetime-of-debt-the-financial- journey-of-the-average-american/** (accessed July 26, 2017).

115. "Inflation," *Investopedia*, **http://www.investopedia.com/terms/i/ inflation.asp** (accessed July 2, 2017).

116. "What are some of the factors that contribute to a rise in inflation?" *Federal Reserve Bank of San Francisco*, (October 2002) **http://www.frbsf.**

org/education/publications/doctor-econ/2002/october/inflation-factors-rise/ (accessed July 2, 2017).

117. "Estate Tax," *IRS*, (October 28. 2016) **https://www.irs.gov/businesses/small-businesses-self-employed/estate-tax** (accessed July 5, 2017).

118. Ashlea Ebeling, "IRS Ruling Helps Surviving Spouses Who Face Estate Tax Trap," *Forbes*, (June 12, 2017) **https://www.forbes.com/sites/ashleaebeling/2017/06/12/irs-helps-surviving-spouses-who-face-estate-tax-trap/#6cdf04387e6f** (accessed July 5, 2017).

119. "U.S. Federal Individual Income Tax Rates History, 1862-2013 (Nominal and Inflation-Adjusted Brackets)," *Tax Foundation*, (October 17, 2013) **https://taxfoundation.org/us-federal-individual-income-tax-rates-history-1913-2013-nominal-and-inflation-adjusted-brackets/** (accessed July 27, 2017).

120. "Women's History in America," *Women's International Center*, **http://www.wic.org/misc/history.htm** (accessed July 7, 2017).

121. Catherine and Richard Greene, "The Man Behind the Magic: The Story of Walt Disney," *Viking Penguin*, New York (1991).

122. Michael Bonny, "5 Businesses Saved by Cash Value Life Insurance," *Paradigm Life*, (March 18, 2015) **http://paradigmlife.net/blog/5-businesses-saved-cash-value-life-insurance/** (accessed August 23, 2017).

123. J. Randy Taraborrelli, "The Hiltons: The True Story of an American Dynasty," *Grand Central Publishing*, New York (April 1, 2014).

124. Joint Committee on Taxation, "General Explanation of the Tax Reform Act of 1986," *99th Congress*, (May 4, 1987) **http://www.jct.gov/jcs-10-87.pdf** (accessed July 7, 2017).

125. Sean Millard, "The US insurance industry: Largest in the world," *Market Realist*, (February 11, 2015) **http://marketrealist.com/2015/02/us-insurance-industry-largest-world/** (accessed August 14, 2017).

126. Barry Dyke, "Cash Value Insurance: A Cornerstone Asset Of a Bank," *InsuranceNewsNet.com*, (November 24, 2008) **http://www.edufunding.com/userfiles/file/Tier%201%20Capital%20and%20Life%20Insurance.pdf** (accessed August 14, 2017).

127. Trent Gillies, "Warren Buffet says indexed funds make the best retirement sense 'practically all the time,'" *CNBC*, (May 14, 2017), **http://www.cnbc.com/2017/05/12/warren-buffett-says-index-funds-make-the-best-retirement-sense-practically-all-the-time.html** (accessed July 8, 2017).

128. Jeff Reeves, "Can an annuity act as your pension plan?" *USA Today*, (April 21, 2016) **https://www.usatoday.com/story/money/personalfinance/2016/04/21/can-annuity-act-your-pension-plan/82768178/** (accessed August 14, 2017).

129. "Companies Use Captives To Fund Pension Benefits," *Treasury & Risk*, (May 2, 2011) **http://www.treasuryandrisk.com/2011/05/02/companies-use-captives-to-fund-pension-benefits** (accessed August 14, 2017).

130. "History of 401(k) Plans: An Update," *Employee Benefit Research Institute*, (February 2005) **https://www.ebri.org/pdf/publications/facts/0205fact.a.pdf** (accessed August 14, 2017).

131. "Compound Annual Growth Rate (Annualized Return)," *MoneyChimp.com*, **http://www.moneychimp.com/features/market_cagr.htm** (accessed August 8, 2017).

Index

About the Author

Leveraging her background as a tax attorney, a Certified Financial Planner® and wealth strategist, Rebecca is uniquely qualified to assess, structure and implement the best income maximization, wealth maximization, tax mitigation/minimization, and optimal legacy strategies for her clients.

Rebecca earned her bachelor's degree, *summa cum laude*, in finance, her Juris Doctor degree, *cum laude*, from the University of Florida, and her advanced law degree in taxation from New York University. Prior to law, she worked for years in finance with Pricewaterhousecoopers LLP and the global networking division of IBM, acquired by AT&T. She continues to practice law in the areas of federal taxation, wealth preservation, trusts and legacy planning, business succession and estate planning, and asset management and protection.

Rebecca spearheads a national practice with clients across the country and enjoys working with high income professionals, business owners, retirees and pre-retirees and high net worth families to implement advanced financial planning and wealth management strategies that maximize income and legacy distribution while minimizing taxes and managing risk. With over 15 years of financial experience, Rebecca capitalizes on her distinctive skillset and years of knowledge to the best advantage of her clients.

Rebecca can be heard nationwide on iHeart radio weekly and she has also been featured in US News & World Report, New York Post, New York Daily News, Yahoo Finance, Bloomberg Business, ABC News, NBC News, CBS News, FOX News, CW, Chicago Tribune, Miami Herald, Boston Globe, LA Daily News, International Business Times, Investing Daily, Street Insider, and numerous other media outlets.

To learn more about the concepts in this book, visit **www.wealth unbroken.com**. To contact Rebecca's practice directly, phone 866.92. WEALTH (866.929.3258), email **info@walserwealth.com**, or visit them online at **www.walserwealth.com**.